Abstract

This book explores real-life situations and scenarios. Examples are drawn upon to explain the 'what's and the why's' after a relationship has broken down.

I have drawn upon my own experiences because I needed to understand why my marriage broke down. More importantly, why the relationship went south so quickly after nearly a decade of emotional investment.

I needed to understand the dynamics of the 'what's and why's.' I additionally needed to understand if there is anything I needed to work on, which caused our separation. Was this connected to something I did in my past, which I have paid for now?

After all, when small infringements occur, many of us tend to brush things under the rug' and think nothing of it. However, what some of us see as small infringements in our relationships may not be insignificant to the other partner; in fact, this minor infringement could be the last thing to make them go over the edge and walk away because of things compiling for a while. Sometimes Karma bites us in the ass when we are not expecting it, to teach us a lesson. However, when things do go wrong this is a time to understand the what's and the why's.

Better than history repeating itself.

When reading this book, read it with an open mind and heart, because otherwise, you may run the risk of miss-learning something crucial that could have helped in a future relationship.

Remember, above all else, if some of us are not learning from our past. Then some of us may make similar mistakes in the future.

Please read intently because there is a lot of valuable insight from our relationship issues that you can learn from.

Perhaps my relationship had to fail, possibly paving the way for future generations to prosper.

Sometimes some of us just need someone or something to happen before we change.

So, perhaps I am that someone and this book is that something!!

And if you are waiting for a sign.

Perhaps this is it!

INTRODUCTION	1
CHAPTER 1 – UNFINISHED CONVERSATIONS OF THE PAST	12
CHAPTER 2 – IDENTITY OF ATTACHMENT ISSUES	26
CHAPTER 3 – UNDERMINING WITHOUT MINING	50
CHAPTER 4 – REJECTION	68
CHAPTER 5 – EXPECTATIONS	89
CHAPTER 6 – MANIPULATING AND LYING	112
CHAPTER 7 – DISILLUSIONMENT OF EROTOMANIAC	133
CHAPTER 8 – SUPPRESSION	158
CHAPTER 9 – THE EMOTIONAL FLOOD GATES	180
CHAPTER 10 – LETTING GO	203
CHAPTER 11 – THE INSECURITIES MANIPULATION THROUGH SUBMISSION	220

CHAPTER 12 – FROM WORRIER TO WARRIOR   245

CHAPTER 13 – COMPULSION, & ABANDONMENT   260

Introduction

The book is focused on identifying issues and problems which may have been overlooked or not identified earlier.

The book also investigates our real-life relationship problems by exploring through the scope of emotional issues.

Each chapter has a different issue or problem which was left unresolved as our marriage came to an end.

I will attempt to gain insight into what went wrong through consulting healers of Wicca, the higher power, Shamans, therapists & counsellors alike, to identify the root cause(s) of why this happened to us.

This book will guide you through a process that I took to rebuild my life after love. Perhaps this may shine a light in the dark place you find yourself in.

Each chapter investigates a different way of healing one's emotional state. The sections are not chronologically connected or interconnected from one to the other, so you can read the chapter(s) that are relevant to you.

The investigational system that will be used to explore the phenomena behind "why things go wrong and what went wrong"; will be the simplest form and will only touch on rudimentary information relevant to the issue.

This book focuses on the problem, and for that reason, we do not elaborate on vast information that leads to a prolonged diagnosis.

The focus here is simplicity.

So, it happened, what I never even dreamt of happening in my wildest dreams. Many of us never look at the things that could potentially go wrong when some of us are in love.

Why would some of us want to do that, when life's fantastic, and some of us find ourselves on top of the world in our unique merry little world, where things are unrealistically perfect.

Until one day, the penny drops!

And one person wants out of the relationship, one day out of nowhere, it's over. Sometimes there are no explanations and those magic words which once brought joy to one's heart; have now brought sorrow. "I love you," turns into, "I don't love you anymore." Those words which we never want to hear are expressed most intensely. I needed an explanation of what happened and who was to blame. The thing is that it all happened in a blink of an eye, for me anyway.

So, I started researching and documenting data that I found, which has turned into this book. I am a sociologist and a criminologist, so, because I study human behaviour, I thought of investigating what happened within my marriage.

What makes this book intriguing is that I am also an empath, so I can sense other people's emotions, and in some cases, I can feel other people's pain. So, this book contains my investigative data explained through exceptional perspectives which have encapsulated ideas and suggestions from Wicca and herbal healers alike.

Sharman's have also been encouraged to give insight on some issues and problems which couldn't be explored through conventional means due to the severity of emotional baggage issues. Which seemed to be connected to unpaid-Karma debts, which, according to the healers, needed to be paid. Which many of us accumulate over a while through our actions, so, seemingly, my Karmic debt was overdue.

Therefore, some of us have karmic debt, and sometimes need to take stock of this; to pay back our dues in life. Because sometimes we need to pay the bill for our actions.

I lost my life partner because this was the price that I had to pay for my karmic debt to be settled. So, reed intently and find out where things went wrong and why; more importantly, you may see something in this book that may salvage your relationship or marriage.

Subsequently, if your reading this book, it may be the case that the worst has happened, and you are trying to put your life back together. This is a chance to perhaps understand situations in the past, which sometimes never made much sense to why it happened.

Maybe through my investigational research may indirectly solve some of your general wanderings!

The mind tidiness can be read by reading any chapter that suits you to get some insight into your emotional state you find yourself in after a break-up and gain some clarity of what happened and why.

However, please try to read the book from beginning to end. As some advice-givers have now perished, and the information contained in this book may never be revealed again.

Read with an open mind; if this book helps, it will bring joy to me knowing that I have made a difference in someone else's life. If it does not, please read it repeatedly until it does as the answers are here.

Healing is not accomplished overnight; after all, it took me seven years just to realize that I wasn't entirely at fault. Imagine what took me seven years could take you as little as weeks or months to gain insight into learning what is not working and why it is not; no one's going to spell it out for you like I am doing here now.

My pain tore through my life like a knife cutting through butter; I experienced the worst pain ever; I needed a friend or someone to turn to, most people turned their backs to me.

"They were always busy from this point on." I would try to find another door soon as one door was slammed shut in my face. This went on for quite a while until I realized 'no one wants to know the broken-hearted.

I remember, I tried to call on friends, those people who seem like the board of directors at times. But I was unlucky, I guess, as they didn't have time for me. I was told, it happens to many people and just to get on with it. One person said have all the potential partners died in the world. "Stop this foolishness and go find someone and leave us alone," another friend's advice.

If you are lucky enough to have friends that care, then remember, dear, you are already healing. Because at this stage, I was still trying to find a shoulder to cry on.

Shall I go on!!

Every time I would recover from one emotional issue, something else would replace it instantly, it was like a never-ending story of painful problems.

I couldn't see the light at the end of my tunnel of life, the walls just closed in, and panic attacks became more and more frequent. I got to the breaking point, where I attempted suicide; due to alienation, aloneness, and depression, I guess I just gave up and wanted it all to be over. From this state, I miraculously recovered, and more importantly,

I educated myself to a high degree while compiling documentation, which has now become this book.

I overcame a great many obstacles in life, from which I thought to write and publish this book containing a lot of emotional insight. But more importantly, it explains what happened and why it happened because although I am healing as I'm writing, I am also documenting so people can use the same method(s) because it has been tried and tested in real-life experiences.

I not only healed, but I believe I have also obtained unique perspectives that have shown me the light through the tunnel of life. My main objective is based on helping people that can't see a way out. Sometimes some of us find that we may not want to talk to anybody. Sometimes we just want to close ranks and just lock ourselves away. I know exactly how some people feel, I went into an emotional prison of my own creation as well.!

Sometimes until the what's and whys have been answered, some of us struggle to cope and move on, I understand this very well because my world had just collapsed too. I needed to know what happened and why it happened. It is said that we learn from our mistakes and other people's stories. So perhaps you can read my story because it's all about the learning and the healing so we can all be well together.

Below, I explain briefly what happened in each chapter, as a different problem is presented in each chapter. From which I will connect a past conversation or something from my relationship to better understand what happened and then find a way to overcome the difficulty. I didn't recognize the signs of the fundamental issues that were unfolding in our marriage until it was too late. Maybe there still might be time to salvage your relationship through what I am about to discuss.

Please read intently, and I hope you find your peace and happiness again.

Anyway, so this is what happened to me.

Chapter 1 – Unfinished conversations of the past

Based on my past conversations, I believe I have ascertained unique perspectives surrounding the above issue. I Believe I have understood my situation a little better since the worst happened by analysing my last marriage. I did this by exploring critical conversations between my partner and me by examining the necessary details that lead up to the collapse of our marriage. I studied the subject above to some detail and used it to understand from this perspective to explore what faults occurred. From which I will explore why it happened and what I could have done to avoid it, and additionally, what I still can do to make sure history does not repeat itself. Some of us learn through experience, and some of us learn from mistakes created by us directly or indirectly. Nevertheless, after the collapse of something that was meant to last the full nine yards. I believe I needed to understand why and what went wrong, so I don't make the same mistake again.

So, here's what happened to me:

This part consists of conversations that have taken place in my past. Moreover, which has left me questioning my morality due to flight responses of the past. There may be parts of this that are interconnected with chapter 23. Therefore, the healing aspects of both chapters are relevant to get success in both issues.

So, here's what happened to me:

The voices in my head are the chatter of the past. Which keeps the past alive in me in the present moment.

This issue really took me to the boundaries of my morality, so I had to get some help, which is outlined below.

I went to a healer,

She informed me that it was not my physical form that needed training.

It was my inner peace that needed to be enhanced.

So, my partner introduced me to guided meditation and hypnosis.

She further informed me of five critical hypotheses,

The first, never leave a situation until you say your peace,

The second, you must now focus on emptying your mind of unfinished conversations (this may be anything which is left unsaid to someone or something which wasn't acted on).

The third, past conversation with your ex's need to be emptied from your mind.

Fourth, think about what they say and answer them accordingly (answers are to be sent to the universe, not necessarily to the person, as the universe will do this for you).

The fifth, realize you are a defender of yourself, and if you find yourself in harm's way, you may defend yourself accordingly, (talk to yourself and make sure you learn this to the letter).

She further said,

First, some of us need to empty your mind and focus on sorting out your mind and your thinking patterns.

Then the lady healer told me a secret, which is listed below!

She said

I appreciate you cannot always say your piece; due to people taking things to the extreme, in which people may result in violence.

So, in some cases, it is best to walk away.

While walking away, keep talking, the conversation in your mind must finish, whether or not the other person hears it or not.

Because your brain needs information which it has gathered to support your argument and when it cannot present the words to the other person(s), the words linger inside the mind.

If this carries on and is left unthreaded, sometimes a person started to talk to themselves, because each conversation needs an end.

She further showed me the way to do this:

Secret step one

Each time something triggers an unfinished conversation, stop, focus on the trigger, and write it down, this is to ensure there's nothing else connected to the trigger.

Secret step two

The unfinished conversation needs to be finished within your mind, you must talk, and say the words as they appear in your mind with an appropriate response for a resolution. (this may stop you thinking about that problem).

Secret step three

Unanswered questions can also bottle up inside; sometimes, people ask questions in which answers may not be given. Sometimes some of us think of an answer later. After the conversation has ended or if some of us flee the area. (Recreate the situation within your mind and send the answers to the universe).

In this instance, say it under your breath or in a private space. You will feel better, and your inner peace will be enhanced.

However, if your mind hasn't come up with an answer or you weren't paying any attention to the question, a solution is not required.

Unless if you think of a solution, then you must present this to the person by visualizing the moment when it happened.

Secret step four

After you have finished an unfinished conversation, then one needs to meditate to bring peace to the chatter of the mind.

It is imperative to meditate through using a mindfulness technique, or otherwise, you run the risk of stockpiling the information.

Secret step five

Detach your triggers which are attached to the unfinished conversation in your mind.

Due to something interconnected with a past ordeal.

Once the trigger has lost its power over you, then one can start to enhance their inner peace.

This is a practice of guided hypnosis; please get a practitioner to aid you; alternatively, everything is free on YouTube.

She further said:

The world will seem more friendly and inviting if you follow the steps with your gut feeling.

Then my partner said. Lastly, I leave you with this:

There is one last thing you need to do.

Forgive your ex's,

This does mean you need to forget the pain and the feelings they put you through.

This also means you are not carrying the brunt of hate around with you anymore.

This lastly needs to be forgiven and move on with your life.

Please take a look at the indicators.

The indicators

1. Conflicted emotions

2. Fear of speaking up

3. Confusion of when to answer

4. Unresolved repetitive flight issues

5. Scared of the aftermath of my words

<u>The solution</u>

1. Overcome conflict issues

2. Overcome fear

3. Become a healthier confident version of one's self

4. Finish the conversation, alone, under one's breath or phone a friend

5. Confidence

6. Speak up

7. Resolve past issues

Tips!!

1. Try something new and exciting, my suggestion tries Yoga - there are 8 different types - try spiritual yoga and experience something which may give you comfort in ways you haven't contemplated just yet.

2. Recycle old emotional baggage - it is like clearing out your old cell phone pictures and old contacts. Somethings that no longer aids us in the future, we simply need to recycle to make room for the new emotional memories that are yet to come.

3. Simplify your life – start focusing on the simpler things and, more importantly, what works for you now. Rather than impress the people, impress yourself by making your life simple.

4. Meditate – listen to nothing, and nothing will control you; listen and refocus your mind and focus by blocking the world out by going into your own world within your mind.

My prayer

Dear GODS, I am healing, and for this, I thank you for your guidance and spirituality of truth through the practice of prayer and meditation.

Chapter 2 – Identity of attachment issues

Based on my past conversations, I believe I have ascertained unique perspectives surrounding the above issue. I Believe I have understood my situation a little better since the worst happened by analysing my last marriage. I did this by exploring critical conversations between my partner and me by examining the necessary details that lead up to the collapse of our marriage. I studied the subject above to some detail and used it to understand from this perspective to explore what faults occurred. From which I will explore why it happened and what I could have done to avoid it, and additionally, what I still can do to make sure history does not repeat itself. Some of us learn through experience, and some of us learn from mistakes created by us directly or indirectly. Nevertheless, after the collapse of something that was meant to last the full nine yards. I believe I needed to understand why and what went wrong, so I don't make the same mistake again.

So, here's what happened to me:

What happened to me was dreadful, but I guess it has to happen to someone, or how else could I tell this story.

Follow openly, please!

I remember a time when nothing mattered; I was 'me.' I had the freedom of choice to do as I pleased.

Then I got older and wiser.

Or did I?

I remember as I grew up, I always tried my best to fit into society, and yet community always seem to reject me because of my far-fetched ideas that went to the ends of the world.

I was creative in a compassionate way; this is, of course, before society knew what creativeness was, so I was just laughed at and never took seriously.

So, as life went on, I saw people dress up, so strangers will pay them attention, as they conformed to their level.

So, I conformed accordingly to fit in, but I didn't care about society, I just wanted to be liked.

I never fit in; I was always the weird one; some people called me a friend at times, so soon as I warmed up to them. They used me to their advantage and then turned the other cheek.

So, I carried on changing thinking the fault lay within me, change after change until I lost my individuality in the ever-growing list of changes. Because I just wanted to fit in with everyone else.

Don't get me wrong; there's nothing wrong with trying to dress the way you want to impress strangers.

However, when one loses their identity trying to become someone else and, in the process, loses their individuality, that is somewhat of a concern.

For example

A while back, I realized that the calibre of women I wanted to be was never going to be in my reach within my present life.

Unless, of course, I changed, it pains me to tell you to what extent I went.

I was so obsessed that I said to myself that 'I would do whatever it took to change my appearance, So I did just that! Without knowing the consequences of course,

From this, I became obsessed with change.

However, I was so lost trying to please others that my individuality was no longer my own.

I didn't care too much, because I had met 'the one' that I was going to marry.

I married my partner; it was short-lived, in any case. I didn't know what to do, because the one I married wanted to know the real me.

So, I started to find myself, and as I went back in time, the one I was married to, realized that my partner could do better as the flood gates opened.

I lost my individuality and my love of my life, and it took several years to get over my partner and find me.

The morel of this is to explain why it's never a good thing to lose one's individuality.

Anyway.

Some of us tend to mimic what other people do in their lives because it may be that some of us like something that works in their life that may also work in our life.

Nothing wrong there, some of us all need to learn new things, but it becomes an issue when some of us try to portray the life of another and, more importantly, inherit not only their persona but their problems and issues too.

My thinking comprised of 'other people has it easy' because I thought their highlights were better than mine. However, highlights of another person's life rarely show, they're behind the scene issues and problems:

Remember:

- A plush person may have – costly issues

- A deprived person may have – underprivileged issues

- A reckless person may have – meaningless issues

- A manipulator may have – identity issues

- A ghastly person may have – unpleasant issues

- A impressionist may have – other people's issues

So, I learned that everyone has problems and issues, they may not have similar problems and issues. But they do have them, and looking from the outside in, one can never see the whole picture. Also, ways remember that be yourself because everyone else is already taken, and change does not mean that you will become someone else. Perhaps in your mind for a while, you may change, but one day that change may inadvertently cost a price you may not be able to pay, as it did with me.

On the other hand, I suppose one could live a life of lies if they believed them, I guess. But do you want to do that?

I couldn't lie, lying started something which cost me a great deal, because lies have a nasty way of coming out at an inappropriate time.

From experience, I am here to inform you that tying solving other people's issues does not solve yours. It doubles the issues and problems.

Time is on no one's side, the time you spend being someone else, means you have even less time to be 'you.'

It is bad enough some of us sell a lot of our time to earn a living, but then what little time some of us have on this earth some of us use unwisely by solving derivative issues and problems.

Become someone special by coming to a better version of yourself.

I learned this the hard way, but none the less, I learned,

Some of us learn by making mistakes, but making derivative mistakes, thinking that you are someone else because you have stepped into their shoes. It is even more time consuming unless, of course, you are artists of lying.

This is not the right mindset to have, because I got to the point where I found myself thinking what others thought.

It got so bad that I started to perceive myself through the perception of what I thought others would understand me as.

- My dress sense changed frequently,

- I watched myself in the mirror daily to pick out different ways to improve me

- I started shopping in the women's section because I thought my partner wanted a person with a clear, bright skin tone.

- Body shaving came into effect, with waxing, which I may add wasn't for me, as I have sensitive skin.

Hahaha

It was laughable.

But yes, that's what I did for love and attachment.

Follow this; it gets weirder from here on in,

The list was endless, but you get the gist, I ended up turning into a 'women' in a man's body, after we broke up, all I attracted was lesbians,

Well,

I guess that had its perks, for a while,

Walking into nightclubs with a girl on each arm seemed to be soothing, I suppose

But when I got home, the lesbians still wanted women, even though they had been coming onto me.

Haha

I was so confused and going out of my mind.

Women through I was cute but gay.

Men thought I was a pushover and used me for my money.

People befriended me just to use me to their advantage because they could see a person who was lost, that had money.

So most people took advantage, people called me brother, (bro), they meant bro as a slang word to say hi and bye.

However, I thought it was someone who cared enough to use the word 'bro' because they excepted me. I was wrong, I would attach myself to them, and they would roll their eyes at me.

So, the moral is, don't copy someone's else character or panache, as you may just inherit their problems too.

I distinctly remember trying to overcome someone else's issues,

Why!

Because I was their clone

I immersed myself in their character and became their clone and gave up who I was.

It took years to unlearn characters that were me, and even longer to battle through there issues, because, once one adopts a problem; the problem becomes a part of you.

Be careful what you mimic.

It is similar to time spent with one's partner; after a while of being together, some of us start to adopt issues from their partner.

Some of us, just pick things up without notice, and this was the case for me, I picked up a lot of issues, problems, and destructive habitual behaviours along the way.

So, it took a while to figure out what was mine and what I had picked up through what I call 'previous attachment accumulator.'

Anyway,

I met a girl who was ghastly to me at the beginning of our part-time relationship and then later warmed up to me, informing me of what people essentially thought of me. And believe me, my partner didn't hold back much. I was traumatized, I remember thinking 'do people go to these extents to use people for money!'

She told me that I was a people pleaser, and people were using me rather than being there for me to be forthright. I would commit suicide because I just couldn't take it any longer. It's a cruel world when you lose your identity and try to please others believe me.

Often some of us don't realize until it's too late. I lost a fair few people that ended up down the path I took.

Then what happened was

After the news spread through the family about my suicide, everyone realized what I was going through wasn't just a rouge to gain attention. And from then on, people started being responsive to my needs and sent me to a specialized identity disorder clinic called rehabilitation clinic.

After the Rehabilitation clinic that I went to, I started to get back to my self slowly but surely.

I managed to gain back my individuality; this took several years, and countless issues, problems, and disorders to overcome, some of which weren't easy to overcome, I assure you.

I learned the lesson in the most challenging way possible.

One thing was for sure when I woke myself up to life,

I found that I was better than all those people that I was trying to be.

And more importantly, I had an inner child that people couldn't understand, because they confused this with weakness, but in fact, it was a surge of will-power that pushed me out of the state that I found myself in.

So, this is what I did throughout my years to gain my power back.

Rather than focus on others – focus on yourself.

Rather than listen to twaddle – listen to something that may benefit you.

Rather than look at fashion – have your own unique rule of the dress.

Rather than follow people – try and develop yourself first.

Rather than attach yourself to another – become independent.

Surround yourself with cheerful, optimistic, and humble people and guess what you will adopt these traits.

Remember

You are the median of the five people you spend time with.

Please take a moment to recognize the indicators that I had, and perhaps you can side-step the potholes of life's unexpected attachment issues, which are yet to come.

Life's never easy, we all need something, but whatever you need in life, remember the five influential people in your life you will be their median. So, pick wisely, or you may run the risk of learning what I had to the most challenging way of them all.

The indicators

1. People pleaser

2. Became someone who, I am not

3. Copycat – mimicking others, mimics their problems too

4. Changing for someone else's benefit, why! Find someone who likes you for you

5. Self-betrayal and Self-sabotaging – never lie to yourself

The solution

1. Look at your future self – write to your future self-explain where you want you to be in 10 years. Don't regret 10 years of missed opportunities. Know where you are going and if you are on track from the word go.

2. Invest in yourself, take a holiday, go somewhere to open the mind to new possibilities, and new experiences can often surprise people of their abilities to overcome the worst issues that they face.

3. Listen to your mind - the mind needs a relaxing time, a time where the reason can think about how to make your work more efficient. The aroma has healing powers that interact with the mind. This is why aromatherapy is excellent to use, along with humidifiers/dehumidifiers and oil defuses. The reason can have some 'me' time, and once it refreshes, you think better and make better decisions.

Tips!!

1. Be happy in the skin you are in

2. Women like different types of men, even our type

3. Learn to be satisfied from within

4. Become you, and remember everyone else is already taken

5. Unlearn people-pleasing! Do you place more emphasis on others' opinions above your own? Do you find yourself helping others overly? Do you feel the need to go that extra mile to help people? Then you are indeed a people pleaser.

6. Work on self-esteem, self-confidence, self-awareness, and self-hurt

<u>My prayer</u>

Forgive me, my GODs, because I haven't accepted 'me.'

even though you created me in your image,

I still somehow decided to parade in someone else's persona.

I truly am sorry for this; please forgive me, as I just want to become 'me,'

After all, it is more fun being myself.

Chapter 3 – Undermining without mining

Based on my past conversations, I believe I have ascertained unique perspectives surrounding the above issue. I Believe I have understood my situation a little better since the worst happened by analysing my last marriage. I did this by exploring critical conversations between my partner and me by examining the necessary details that lead up to the collapse of our marriage. I studied the subject above to some detail and used it to understand from this perspective to explore what faults occurred. From which I will explore why it happened and what I could have done to avoid it, and additionally, what I still can do to make sure history does not repeat itself. Some of us learn through experience, and some of us learn from mistakes created by us directly or indirectly. Nevertheless, after the collapse of something that was meant to last the full nine yards. I believe I needed to understand why and what went wrong, so I don't make the same mistake again.

So, here's what happened to me:

Without realizing it, I let my partner train me indirectly into submission. I didn't acknowledge the end result until it was too late. The more I played the game, the more issues and disorders seem to attach themselves to me. Sometimes even games can turn into conditions; the problems happened after my partner disappeared. This particular game we played created neediness issues in me and issues of control in my ex-partner.

It was fun at the beginning, in many ways, it became our thing; the problem was I became dependable on my partner. And my partner, on the other hand, started to influence me indirectly.

Each time I made a healthy choice, my partner would say the following!

"Are you sure."
"Are you sure, honey."
"Are you sure, do you want a second to re-think."
"Are you sure, honey."

If a persisted with my answer.

My partner would touch me, feel me, cress me, and when I'm aroused, pull away; intimacy was used as a bargaining chip.

Some partners can't resist the advances of their partner and sometimes end up in submission, as I frequently did.

For my partner, this was just a game, and for me, the game turned into a life choice because soon after, I started to second guess my every decision.

As I slowly declined into submission of giving in, my partner took advantage of my caving's and would later manipulate my every decision. It was just a case of my partner being more knowledgeable than me.

She became a stronger and resilient woman, whereas I started to doubt every decision and became a needy reliant individual, and this turned into a struggle to win arguments, as my partner always seemed to have the upper hand.

It took a while to identify why I lost more than most disputes with my partner, but this only came into realization when we split up.

Soon as my partner input and data weren't in my mind, that's is when I realized something wasn't quite adding up.

After a while, with the help of professional guidance, I came to terms with my disorder and started to understand why I was thinking the way I was.

This also manifests into insecurity issues, which would further start displaying traits of paranoia because second-guessing became second nature to me.

The more I tried to overcome a situation; the more problems became apparent. It got so bad that OCD indicators started occurring from which I began to struggle with habitual behaviours.

After weeks of therapy, I realized that I needed to stop this disorder faster.

SO, I found a healer,

Who said

I needed to stop watching TV."

I said

"Oh God, not TV."

She said

"This is no joke."

I said

"Please help, I will pack up the TV when I get home."

I mean, I would have given my partner the TV if my partner could fix me.

Why TV? I asked my partner!

Funny enough,

Because I was adding to the disorder,

I needed to replace watching TV with will feel-good films.

Why!

Because the TV controls us collectively where some of us know it or not.

So, if the TV wants to undermine us, it brings us to a state whereby some of us conform to the TV's ideas. Rather than follow our path.

The healer also said

When you watch a positivity film, the mind records this and slowly wrights a new program for us to better function.

The healer asked me to do something significant before watching films,

She wanted me to write lively letters by hand to myself. And each letter had to be printed 5 times repeatedly.

I asked

"Why"

She said

"The mind needs to build a programming language, which the mind will use to write your new mind program."

I said

"I don't understand."

She said

"When you write positive letters to yourself repeatedly, your mind starts to learn what mindset you are after."

"And soon starts to compile the language, in which it is going to build your new thought pattern."

This would soon bring my mind to a holt. And to some extent, it gives me the ability to trust myself again.

Soon as I started to trust myself and trust that I was making informed, correct decisions, I started focusing on single disorders rather than tackle the whole issue collectively.

Herbal healing worked for me, and their practitioners are more knowledgeable of any professional today.

So, I started down a path that bought me to the finish line quickly and faster than any professional institute.

Because herbal healers do not use addictive medicine to heal, when the healer was treating me, my partner improved the issue, not like professionals nowadays who give you a further few problems, which are commonly known side effects.

Each problem, disorder, and issue that I would identify, the healer would give me a set herbal healing solution to overcome it.

Rather than get the pills with addictive drugs from the physicians

I relied on herbal medicine; after all, what physicians prescribed started with herbal medicine, but they add the addictive drugs, which, of course, bring repeat business to them.

I did not want to give them repeat business. But I have to say, in defence of the professionals, they do a great job and help millions upon millions of people.

So, please do not come off your medicines by reading this book. The only time you should consider swopping is when your doctor and herbal healer can do the exchange for you.

I started to recover from a disorder every two months. I used a small number of drugs from my physician, which did not work for me, because I could feel the drug-taking over. So I went above to herbal healing at a very early stage, and herbal solution started to work for me faster.

The indicators

1. I stopped trusting my gut feeling

2. Insecurity issues

3. Compulsive and habitual thoughts

4. Overthinking

5. Doubting myself

6. Trust issues

<u>The solution</u>

1. Respect your doubts, - they are there to help

2. Listen to one's gut feeling

3. Other people's opinions do not matter

4. Know your morals

5. Trust yourself

6. Become your own best friend

7. Listen to your inner critic

8. Stop overthinking

9. Meditation

Tips!!

1. Self-love, I have said this before, and I'll repeat it. Self-love means that you acknowledge your triumph. When you feel like you have accomplished enough, pat yourself on the back and appraise yourself for a job well done. Shake your own hand and high-five yourself. And if that isn't enough to look in the mirror and tell yourself that you're the right person and you have done a brilliant job. Admiring yourself in this manner simply means that you don't need others' opinions in your life. And more importantly, you love yourself. It might be an unorthodox way of doing something, and not to mention weird. But sometimes some of us need the appraisal of others. So why don't you

give it to yourself rather than wait for other people to do just that? If somebody else appraises you, then that indeed is a plus too.

a. My point is basically this, don't wait for other people to give you praise for your work. Once you have given a appraise to yourself, then the ball starts rolling. I used to hold my breath, seeking the first appraisal. However, when a critic would say something negative, the feeling inside would just bring me down to my knees. This way of appraising yourself no second negative opinion of somebody else can do just that, remember that above all else!

2. Recycle old emotional baggage – it is like clearing out your old cell phone pictures and old contacts. Somethings that no longer aids us in the future, we simply need to recycle to make room for the new emotional memories that are yet to come.

3. Simplify your life – start focusing on the simpler things and, more importantly, what works for you now. Rather than impress the people, impress yourself by making your life simple.

4. Meditate – listen to nothing, and nothing will control you; listen and refocus your mind and focus by blocking the world out by going into your own world within your mind.

My prayer

My GODS, only you know the ride of life that I went through, I am so glad that you were beside me every step of the way.

From my experience, perhaps you could make sure this book finds its way to those who need to overcome what I have.

So, here's what happened to me:

To better understand rejection, I have broken it down into three categories:

1. Past rejections which explore my old relationships;
2. Present rejections, this explores my current fear of rejection
3. Future, which I see with a negative outlook due to basing this on my past experiences.

Past rejection =partner rejected

What haunts me from time to time; it is my partner, stating that I will end up alone.

However, my partner also contradicts oneself when my partner says,

"don't worry, you will find someone else."

What does that mean other than the obvious?

Each time we would have a disagreement, my partner would come out with these lines and follow through with how much my partner doesn't love me; for some reason or another, my partner would work out a percentage of how much my partner didn't love me and then joke about it.

After the humour was over, I remember I nearly always felt this deep affliction within, like something didn't add up. I failed to identify the root cause of why my partner would say such things. I mean, some of us were in a relationship, weren't we?

No matter what I gave up former partner, it was never enough, as my partner wanted something else to change.

My partner would laugh in my face each time I asked my partner why my partner was taunting me.

She would say, "your ex-partners left you, and done better than you, so, I am going to follow suit."

" I remembered the first time I said "NO" to my partner demands; it was shocking; to say the least, I finally felt like a human being; my partner was so annoyed that my partner stormed out.

I sometimes regret not standing up for myself sooner; I guess when some of us think some of us are in love, some of us tend to overlook the factors of control.

Sometimes some of us want to fit into another's persons perfect picture that some of us forget what it is some of us actually want out of the relationship.

We need to slow down before some of us lose the sense of who some of us are,

Well,

I needed to, because, looking back, it wasn't our life, it was my partner life, and I just fit in, when I couldn't fit in, I was no longer a part of it. I don't think there was an 'us' in the end.

Don't get me wrong we had some magical memories, but the fact of the matter was that some of us were never compatible, and the connection that some of us had was based on my people-pleasing skills.

The day I stopped pleasing my partner, that was the day my partner walked out and sent the papers through the post for divorce.

The morel of this story is, remember to be yourself in whatever situation you find yourself in. This is of paramount importance.

Don't be captivated in another person's life that you forget to live your own.

Life is a commitment from the GODS. However, when some of us falter. Some of us are hurting our self's because we may not be living up to our potential.

Live life and those who are supposed to be a part of the journey will stay in your life; those who are not a part of your journey will one day walk away.

No matter how much some of us want people to be a part of our lives, that is a choice some of us can't make, unfortunately.

Some of us try to fit into someone else's perception of life because some of us don't want to lose them; life is simple; let it be just that.

The right person on your path will come soon as you let go of the toxic relationship, which is not making you happy at all.

I held on to my partner because I couldn't see the future of my goals.

Present rejection – fear of rejection

As I move forward, move forward alone at that; trying to heal myself to some degree, I feel like each woman that I come across is pre-judging me, in the sense that I see my partner plotting for how long my partner wants to keep me. I realize it is a crazy notion to have. It may be a defence mechanism because of insecurity issues.

It may even be the case that I set myself up for a fall, each time I am connected with another woman.

I had such a romantic side, because of my partner's daddy issues, my partner would ruin any heartfelt surprises and romantic gestures that I planned.

Although I would remember each occasion and prepare it in advance. My partner wouldn't even remember my birthday. But I still loved my partner, even when I felt inside so much pain.

Imagine someone telling you that they could have done better than you.

Imagine someone telling you that they thought of you as a joker and never could respect you.

Imagine someone telling you that they could replace you merely by the click of my partner fingers.

Imagine hearing that several times a week, for nearly a decade, what would myself worth feel like???

She broke me and then kicked me to the curb, like a piece of garbage. my partner never even looked back, even after my suicide attempt, my partner never ever looked back after hearing about it.

So, when I see the prospects of a loving relationship with someone, I also see myself being kicked to the curb.

Future rejection - pre fear rejection will come.

Sometimes, I see a possible future with a wife and kids, we live in a house with a white picket fence in a nice neighbourhood.

And I am full of life and energy as I live with someone who loves me. Then I wake up and realize it was only a dream.

I find myself walking around, telling girls that I love them. Some girls run a mile, and others laugh at me.

I do this because I want to bypass that point where some of us decide where or not my partner likes me.

I want the magic that other people have on the holidays. Instead, a lonely Christmas is what I have since 2012. It seems, the harder I try, the more difficult it is, trying to find my other half.

Some people say to me, "move on," I mean, "With whom."

I find myself on many social media sites, and soon as I open my heart, all they see is a needy man.

If I don't open my heart, then I am an emotional snob.

Sometimes, some of us try too much while others try not enough, and some of us have the bad luck of bumping into people that have either been working too hard in a relationship in which case they are laid back and may seem uninterested.

And the other which haven't tried enough in their past relationship, so they try too hard and come off being needy and desperate.

If one gets off to a start, then, of course, there is the issue of what baggage they may be carrying.

For instance, they may have met people that either haven't been hurt in love or who have.

A wise person once said, "don't wait because there will never be a right time."

The wise person forgot to say "will it last or not"

After seeing many romantic films and episodes, I realize that a relationship needs constant attention from both individuals if it is to blossom.

The moral here is never to try too much in a relationship. Try enough, and watch the other person invest in the relationship just as much as you. Because this way, some of us have something to build on.

However, if you prefect everything, then there will be nothing to improve on, and the relationship will no doubt fall into a routine, which can end up in boredom valley. Where nothing happens, and people end up either conforming to the new reality, or they separate from the routine of boredom.

Take on the rein and hand the other one to the partner, as a responsibility shared or halved is a problem shared.

Respect and trust are a commodity that can never be broken, and if they are, they can never be repaired. These are the foundations of any lasting relationship. Please never lie, because lies are the cracks that appear in a lasting relationship.

The lie is like the snake when it stings. The effects are devastating, sometimes even life-threatening.

The main point is too set out the terms of what you want and find out what my partner wants. And then set out date in the future (five years) whereby any partner can bring forward a revised referendum. This way 'promises' are not set in stone; because face it as we get older, we all change in one way or another, and what once worked may not work. Because we live in an ever-changing world so, promises should be open to change too.

Perhaps even a renewal of vowels whereby a person can opt-out of marriage maybe every 10 years. Because the world that we live in is complicated in many ways. And committing to somebody fully in an ever-changing world basically means to some people that they may have set in stone their entire life based on a prior commitment. Thus, the common saying, "I was young dumb and stupid or just hopelessly in love with the possibility of a happy ever after.

Being that most of us have excepted gay marriages, I think going forward, we should acknowledge the fact that people need a break at some point too. In the union to realize is the change in character really fits the person they want to be with, it's just that sometimes we have grown apart from one another and want different things.

It does pain me to say this, but if it's meant to be and both parties want to spend the entirety of their life with another, then indeed renewal dates are nothing to worry about. It would save money on divorce imagine. Not to mention, some people may have tried even and earth to keep in the other good graces.

Well, I think that is a conversation for another time.

Hahaha

The indicators

1. Making assumptions of other thoughts

2. Trusting people with your feelings

3. Compromising may be difficult

4. The worriedness of letting people in

5. People-pleasing? Do you place more emphasis on others' opinions above your own? Do you find yourself helping others overly? Do you feel the need to go that extra mile to help people? Then you are indeed a people pleaser.

6. I feel like I am not worthy of love

7. I have a hard time believing people love me

8. My expectations are of grand gestures rather than be in the moment

9. I set myself up for a fall

The solution

1. Stop haemorrhaging with the past

2. Learn how to connect with people

3. Revive your self-worth and self-respect

4. Stop trying to please the world

5. Stop trying to impress others with grand gestures

6. Live in the moment

7. Access potential changes which you are comfortable with

8. Expect and assume nothing

9. Be yourself

Tips!!

1. Live in the moment

2. Trust that there is someone out there for me

3. Stop people-pleasing

4. Expect and assume nothing

5. Be my own best friend

6. Revive my self-worth and self-respect

My prayer

Dear GODS, I have healed so much, thank you, hopefully, you can point me in the right direction, I really hate rejection.

Hopefully, I won't get too much of it, as I am in the process of self-perfecting myself in terms of being me, the best version that I can.

The past has now gone, and I am coming to terms with the present, but I must admit I still fear the future as it is uncertain as of yet, please look after me, dear GODS, thank you.

Chapter 5 – Expectations

Based on my past conversations, I believe I have ascertained unique perspectives surrounding the above issue. I Believe I have understood my situation a little better since the worst happened by analysing my last marriage. I did this by exploring critical conversations between my partner and me by examining the necessary details that lead up to the collapse of our marriage. I studied the subject above to some detail and used it to understand from this perspective to explore what faults occurred. From which I will explore why it happened and what I could have done to avoid it, and additionally, what I still can do to make sure history does not repeat itself. Some of us learn through experience, and some of us learn from mistakes created by us directly or indirectly. Nevertheless, after the collapse of something that was meant to last the full nine yards. I believe I needed to understand why and what went wrong, so I don't make the same mistake again.

So, here's what happened to me:

No matter what I have tried, everything in the end fails, and I usually end up with nothing. Is it bad luck, or am I the percentage of people in life destined to fail?

It is like the harder I try the more challenging life gets; even when I give up, life still seems to kick me, like I am being punished for a crime from my past life or something on that level.

Why me,

See this happened a lot in my life, it's like some higher power had made its mind that I was the one that was always nearly going to make it and soon as I can foresee my goals being achieved someone or something or some force of nature swoops in and takes everything.

On occasion, I do have the misfortune of doing all the work, and instead of appreciation, I end up with someone blaming me for something or another.

It's got to that point where I just put my hand up and take the blame, whether I have done something wrong or not because some people blame me in the end anyway.

So, I told an acquaintance what had been going on in my life, and they were not surprised. I distinctly remember them saying, "you should have sought help a while ago, long before the issues piled up."

I just started weeping, as I had reached the end of my tether,

My acquaintance informed me they knew of a wise man who could help me, I must admit I was intrigued, but more so that I was ready to try anything.

So, my acquaintance gave me the contact details to this wise man, and I was later to meet with this person.

I was a bit dubious, but at the time, I remember feeling optimistic about the wise man because he was about to show me another way to deal with my ever-amounting issues.

So, I went off to see the wizard of Oz, down the yellow brick road.

Haha,

I remember thinking of Dorthey in the Wizard of Oz,

I thought I was going to get all the answers that I was seeking,

But is it ever that simple!!

Well, this is what the wizard, I mean, the wise man said!!

"think before you act."

I said, "THINK, THINK, THINK, THAT'S ALL I EVER DO," in a fit of rage.

The wise man then said

"think some more."

I said THINK

Haha, that's all I ever do, wise-man, I said

The wise man then said

"Think about what you will do; what you are about to do; does it benefit you or someone else."

I was stomped, So, I said whatever do you mean wise man, I wanted to say, old man. Hahaha

The wise man then said, listen carefully,

"think if you take the whole task on alone; then when things go wrong, there's only one person to blame."

I said, "when I share the task, I am overlooked, and someone takes the rewards; I am taking the blame when I am not overlooked."

The wise man said, "it is your expectations of bad luck, and you have a negative mindset."

And then said

"you are looking for that thing that goes wrong in everything, and thus, you set yourself to fail."

Followed by:

"think positive and positive things will happen to you."

I was intrigued, so I stayed quiet and only said, "please, sir carry on."

The wise man then followed with;

"stop looking for the negative in the positive and start looking for the positive in the negative."

I was stomped, but at the same time, things looked brighter, as I felt I had gained some invaluable insight/knowledge into what I was emotionally feeling.

It was like I mattered again, and something was helping me move forward rather than hold me back.

The more I looked for the positive in the negative, the more things just started to materialize for me.

It was like a miracle that had taken place.

So, I was feeling great,

Finally, things were moving forward.

As I was about to leave the wise man, a thought dawned upon me.

I thought to get my times worth, so, I asked further advised because I struggled at that time to make friends.

I mean, each time I make a friend, something went wrong, and I ended up alone.

Was it me, was it the colleague from work who turned into a friend!! Or should I not bother to make friends.

So, I ask the wise man if he could shed some light on what was going on.

He said:

"break the vicious circle of negativity, you are not to make friends at work, these are your work colleagues and nothing more, friendships take time to build with mutual trust and respect."

And then he said:

"real friendships happen without effort, don't be in a rush to make friends, because you may end up with 'users' rather than friends."

Followed by:

"stop listing to twaddle and start listing to yourself."

He then said STOP

Followed by:

"slow down and keep one eye on your goals, and the other eye on your actions."

"Beware, you never walk looking backward, so don't focus behind, focus on the road ahead."

He then said something that boggled me somewhat.

He said:

keep your other eye on the bigger dreams, which are soon will be in your grasp!"

I said

"That's three eyes, I have only two.

He said

"then open your third eye and see the world."

He followed with

"no wonder you are not grasping the bigger dreams, you can't even see what's right in front of you."

At this stage, I was willing to try anything,

so I opened my third-eye,

through many hours of guided meditation.

It was not an easy process, but that is a story for another time.

After I opened my third eye, I realized and understood things on a much higher level from which I have started to move up in different ways.

Sometimes I feel cheated because if I had opened my third eye sooner, perhaps, I would not have had so much sorrow and pain in my life.

The wise man stated;
"It is only through sorrow and pain that bought you to me; why else would you come to me."

Then said,
"Everyone has time to wake up their third eye,

More importantly,

you have to be ready to understand this power, it is not merely a case of opening it earlier, it opens when the time is right for you".

"Become, stronger, become wiser, become you."

"Never look back, and never look too far ahead, stay in the here and now with a plan in mind. Be the creator of your destiny and move down your path with no struggles."

"Struggles are for the foolish and hurtful, not for you."

"Finally, remember to do something wrong time to time, this will show you how far you have come, and show you that there is no positive without negative."

There needs to be a 50% balance of positive and negative, remember to look for the positive in the negative."

The indicators

1. Expecting too much

2. Expecting something in return

3. Expecting change through struggles

4. Becoming entwined with negative emotions

5. Feeling trapped

6. Thinking there's no way out

7. Panicking

8. Control freak

9. Setting ones self-up for failure

The solution

1. Self-belief

2. Learn how to think before actions

3. If in doubt stop, slow down and think what to do next

4. Overcome overthinking

5. Don't try to take on the world

6. Expect nothing in return by doing someone a good deed

7. Take compliments,

8. Worry less, of possible outcomes, remember they are only potential and can be changed if your reaction to the problem changes.

Tips!!

1.   Connect obsession with humour – each time you find yourself obsessing, humour yourself and think why, and how long you have been doing this for. Put a time on the obsessing

1.   Self-love, I have said this before, and I'll repeat it. Self-love means that you acknowledge your triumph. When you feel like you have accomplished enough, pat yourself on the back and appraise yourself for a job well done. Shake your own hand and high-five yourself. And if that isn't enough to look in the mirror and tell yourself that you're the right person and you have done a brilliant job. Admiring yourself in this manner simply means that you don't need others' opinions in your life. And more importantly, you love yourself. It might be an unorthodox way of doing something, and not to mention weird. But sometimes some of us need the appraisal of others. So why don't you give it to yourself rather than wait for other people to do just that? If somebody else appraises you, then that indeed is a plus too.

2. My point is basically this, don't wait for other people to give you praise for your work. Once you have given a appraise to yourself, then the ball starts rolling. I used to hold my breath, seeking the first appraisal. However, when a critic would say something negative, the feeling inside would just bring me down to my knees. This way of appraising yourself no second negative opinion of somebody else can do just that, remember that above all else!

3. Unhinge your **FEARS**, because sometimes some of us can become unpredictable throughout emotions. Sometimes wants and needs can be confused, and sometimes some of us can take out our inner desires, on the wrong person from which sometimes some of us regret things that some of us do in the spur of the moment. Listen to your gut feeling and stop yourself from fearing different social

situations. It is those uncomfortable situations that create room for fear. Face your fear before your fears face you.

4. Empty mindfulness issues of society in your mind, what people believe only may work for them, so meditate and clear out the emotional garbage of being alone before your ready.

5. Talk to a medical professional or a friend, talking is the best therapy as it helps us to realize the inner baggage that some of us burden ourselves with. Those embarrassing moments that some of us never share with the world until it's too late. Don't let the Pied Piper blow your trumpet for after the worst has passed. Let go of the past by either writing things in a journal or telling someone about what has happened.

6. Get back on your own track – or you run the risk of not meeting your destiny.

7. Simplify your life – start focusing on the simpler things and, more importantly, what works for you now. Rather than impress the people, impress yourself by making your life simple.

My prayer

GODS of GODS, One love and peace to all!!!

Dear GODS, please keep showing me the way, as I still sometimes find the negativity in the positive. Please, lords, guide me through the negativity and show me the buoyant torch through the thick mist of negativity.

Dear GODs, please help me overcome social issues that prevent me from enjoying myself.

Also. Please GODS if you are listing, help me, I don't want to be alone, not anymore, I want to be in a relationship with someone leading to marriage and start a family. I don't want to be alone, I

Thank you, my GODS, for your guidance you have given me through this awkward time.

Please help me to finish my book(s), which will incidentally solve most of my problems in my life.

Thank you and bless my Gods.

A message to all my ex-partners, girlfriends, and one-night stands. I am sorry for anything I have done or haven't done; I have suffered the wrath of karma for over a decade now. Please, forgive me as I have forgiven you.

Chapter 6 – Manipulating and lying

Based on my past conversations, I believe I have ascertained unique perspectives surrounding the above issue. I Believe I have understood my situation a little better since the worst happened by analysing my last marriage. I did this by exploring critical conversations between my partner and me by examining the necessary details that lead up to the collapse of our marriage. I studied the subject above to some detail and used it to understand from this perspective to explore what faults occurred. From which I will explore why it happened and what I could have done to avoid it, and additionally, what I still can do to make sure history does not repeat itself. Some of us learn through experience, and some of us learn from mistakes created by us directly or indirectly. Nevertheless, after the collapse of something that was meant to last the full nine yards. I believe I needed to understand why and what went wrong, so I don't make the same mistake again.

So, here's what happened to me:

Part one: Understand why some of us lie

I use to work as a sales executive, and manipulating people in to a sale was a forte of any salesperson, even me, as one needed this tool to access ways to influence the customer into surrendering themselves into a sale. Not to mention, fast-tracking the customer through a swift sale process by suppressing the need to know trivial information, due to key performance indicators (KPIs) and target driven sales.

So, basically,

To lie to a person's face and be taken at face value, was a job requirement,

We were taught to place a lie over a lie, this prevents the underlying lie from going undetected. So, in essence, a person believes the lies they are telling to be the truth.

Let me elaborate: if you find yourself in a particular situation whereby you need to lie to your partner, or perhaps want to know if someone may be lying to you. Take a read below!

A liar steps.

Face it, some of us need to lie on occasion! Even if it is a white lie.

Scenario, you may have cheated on your partner; and now you regret it; and you need a quick fix; before your partner fixes you. You're in a panic, and you need a way out of a tricky situation. Believe me when I say the following, do not do this, try not to cheat, and try not to lie, you will damage the trust between your partner and yourself, it will be like a bomb going off in your foundation of your relationship. Believe me it will be devastating; it may even topple your relationship. However, if you still want to go forward with the lie, follow the steps below:

The following is primarily based on a man cheating on a woman:

Because some men are cheaters:

1. Talk to any woman, and say "no, no, no," then go and have a alcoholic drink.
2. Do the above five times.
3. Then, talk to a further 5 women, and say "I love my partner" then go and have a alcoholic drink each time. This will slowly take away the guilt away.
4. Then get drunk, to the point of black out,

5. Soon as you get home, the conversation will prominently be based over the state you have arrived back in.

6. Change the topic of questions and complain that you were in a drunken state ,and your friends left you at some point, say "I can't believe it" multiple times, then start to weep.

7. In the morning, when asked, what happened, lie with the intent to get caught a few times.

8. Such as the amount of alcohol you had and keep empathizing on how you were legless. "Never remember a thing is key, it's a blur."

9. And how you made a fool out of yourself by dancing with anybody and everybody.

10. Use humour and keep evading the topic by reiterating the fun you had.

11. Most importantly, always stick to a short and straightforward story and empathize with amnesia.

12. Never mention names, places, or times. Those are the things that will get you caught out. The key words are, it's a blur, can't remember much.

13. Keep iterating the word "sorry" your partner will assume that you are sorry for the state you have come back in, but really, you are apologising for cheating on them.

If you believe that's all that happened, then that's is what your partner will think too. Your partner will expect a lie, and you haven't disappointed.

It is the same with a customer; you explain to yourself that there are no defects to what you are selling with a straight face, and people will believe you at face value.

The problem is, once you get home, the lying starts there too, as it did with me, and I would manipulate any conversation to aid in my victory even if it meant lying to my partner.

It was so good that I won lost arguments.

It was funny and exciting until my partner caught on.

I guess my partner was naïve, not foolish.

It hurts when it happens to you, believe me, the only difference with us was we destroyed our foundations because we never addressed it, rather we both did it in the end as it just became something, we did to one another, I suppose.

A marriage based on lies is not a marriage: as the most prominent factor disappears 'trust,' and soon as that happened,

well,

the foundations of our relationship crumbled, and down came everything that some of us spent so long building.

Part two: learn from the hurt, don't keep hurting yourself.

I never lie now, not even a white lie, because it wasn't worth it in the end.

What I am trying to say, do what you have to, but soon as you come through your front door, leave the bullshit outside.

The lies lead to other issues, and we never recovered the trust soon as it was broken.

Because, before you trust anyone, you have to respect them, and we couldn't respect one another. After that, all we had was two people who use to love each other, and now they are strangers once more. It is essential never to lie, no matter what you have done, nothing worse than a liar.

After we broke up, so many deceivers and liars crossed my path,

It was like the Gods were teaching me a lesson,

I vividly recall a dream; the Gods spoke to me and said: "be a liar; then these are the people that will surround you."

I quit my job, and started on the path of redemption, but the lesson was learnt too late as our marriage dissolved. All that was left was an amount of emotion issues, problems and heartache, because of bad choices.

The Gods further foretold me, "a lairs redemption is not merely based on a sorry, the punishment for this, arrives in small doses until you see the errors that you create".

I listened to that dream and changed my views of life.

Part three: Lying without the intent to:

I make it a point to never lie; it is not easy as sometimes a lie can help a situation better than the truth, for example, reverse psychology – when you don't want someone to do something, you ask them to do it anyway. Because sometimes people want to do the opposite of what one is explaining to them.

However, the lie takes shape when some of us try to manipulate people in thinking some of us have done something when indeed, some of us haven't.

If this happens, the wording needs to address the truth, follow the examples set out below:

1.   Rather than say you did it – replace it with – I did it my way – then connect the lie to this. Technically you haven't been particular, thus resulting in no lie.

2.   Rather than say it is good or bad – replace it with – I think it needs some work

3.   If asked what time you did something, tell the time before you did the last thing before you did this thing. Confusing is better than a lie.

4.   If someone asks you the date of when it happens – say "the day before last | and then follow by "or was it last week in the last day or

the day before the last day" – the person will be confused, trying to find out which day you are talking about. Again, no lie.

But try not to lie, because it hurts when someone lies to you.

When you tell the truth, it remains the truth to matter how many different ways it is said.

However, when someone is lying, one must remember which lie you told to who.

This is why times, dates, and places are hard to remember, so use one form of reference or quote which clears up doubt and the question in the same instance.

The more you confuse the person, the more the questions stop, because face it, no one wants to look stupid.

Also, overload people with information about something that happened to someone else. Because their perception of reason starts to falter somewhat.

The indicators

1. Compulsive liar - Pity parties – 'everyone should stop off their life journey and help me,' 'life's not worth living' – are the thoughts of pitying one's self. Beware, a pity party can turn into something more serious such as detachment from the world and lead one into alienation and suicide. Be careful how you think; as thoughts can turn into actions. As they did with me.

1. Manipulator of truth - Comparing my life with others – this is silly, everyone's on a journey of their own. Aid in comfort that someone who isn't in your life anymore; there part in your journey is over, time to move on. Who knows you may meet again along the road which is uncertain that lies ahead?

2. Fear – we all have this, we all need this, it keeps us safe from the uncertainties of the unfamiliar situations, learn to embrace it rather than fear it.

3. Thoughts of loneliness, lonesome and loner – learn to be happy alone, only then your life lesson is achieved and only

then you can make another 'happy,' rather than rely on a partner, more so, and push them away through neediness.

4. Irritable, inner anger – for not being attractive, can lead to severe pursuits of one's appearance.

5. Grandiose – one feels that they are pretentiously important in something or someone's life.

6. Emotionally detached, it was crazy, I remember, those days where time would stop when some of us held each other. some of us were inseparable, and now some of us barely looked at each other.

The solution

1. Trust your judgment - brainwashing is the best way to recover from alienation – this is done by taking a break and moving somewhere where one can focus on themselves where the routine of normality is far, and something new can open the mind up.

2. Try not to fit in - In some cases, mindfulness can help - it is a form of meditation healing that can clear the mind of intrusive thoughts, patterns of abnormal behaviour in adults, and, more importantly, remove habitual behaviours that are linked to such disorders as OCD. Where one becomes detached from the world.

3. Stop compromising - guided hypnosis can help to aid in bringing one's confidence up and gaining some self-awareness of the real-world outside the realms of normal perceptions.

6. Listen to your gut feeling.

Tips!!

1. Rationalization - A holiday, somewhere to open the mind to new possibilities, and new experiences can often surprise people of their abilities to overcome the worst issues that they face.

2. Talk less and listen more - Stop late nights – late nights puts an unimaginable stress on the mind, because nights are when the mind makes heads and tales of your issues in the day. So, sleep earlier and gain a better prospective in the morning.

3. Match my actions with my words - Aromatherapy – The mind needs relaxing time; a time where the mind can think about how to make you work more efficiently. The aroma has healing powers that interact with the mind. This is why aromatherapy is great to use, along with humidifiers/dehumidifiers and oil defuses, as they work well with aroma oils. The mind can have some 'me' time and once it refresh's, you think better and make better decisions.

4. Never lie - stop late nights – late nights put an unimaginable stress on the mind, because nights are when the mind makes heads and tales of your issues in the day. So, sleep earlier and gain a better prospective in the morning.

5. Never lie - listen to forests, wale, and soothing sounds to ease the chatter of the mind. This helps bring the mind to attention, the mind needs time to process the daily downloaded information from what you observe and learn and of course what you stress about.

6. Never lie - Write or compile your worries in words on paper, like I have done in some parts of this book. The words you write have power; think Shakespeare words still have meaning in our life's. From which some of us adapt our life's each day, from which some of us learn and become better. So, in

essences some of us are doing just the same, some of us are healing through writing down our worries and pain as did Shakespeare. Because face it, even Shakespeare was in pain. If he didn't write some of us as a race of humans would have missed so much. So, pick up a pen and paper and get them thoughts down and let go of what was.

My prayer

Bless me, my Gods and Goddesses, I have manipulated people into submission; I wasn't aware that `I was doing it some of the time, and other times, I didn't know what manipulation was other than undermining some people.

Chapter 7 – Disillusionment of erotomaniac

Based on my past conversations, I believe I have ascertained unique perspectives surrounding the above issue. I Believe I have understood my situation a little better since the worst happened by analysing my last marriage. I did this by exploring critical conversations between my partner and me by examining the necessary details that lead up to the collapse of our marriage. I studied the subject above to some detail and used it to understand from this perspective to explore what faults occurred. From which I will explore why it happened and what I could have done to avoid it, and additionally, what I still can do to make sure history does not repeat itself. Some of us learn through experience, and some of us learn from mistakes created by us directly or indirectly. Nevertheless, after the collapse of something that was meant to last the full nine yards. I believe I needed to understand why and what went wrong, so I don't make the same mistake again.

So, here's what happened to me:

As far back as I can remember, I have always been disappointed in one way or another. Perhaps just bad luck, I suppose! Or was it something more heinous at work; I mean, I strive going forward in life, but continuously something just goes sour, and I end up on the brunt end of things. I mean, if it happens a couple of times, we can only say "that was unfortunate"; if it happens a few times, we can just say "that was bad luck." But every time I tried to strive in life, something goes pear-shaped. It is like I can see something going wrong. And no matter how hard I try; something disrupts the pattern of success somehow.

It didn't matter what it was that I was unsuccessful at because the more times I was unsuccessful, the more times I would try until I was successful. But each time I had this lingering thought in the back of my head, saying to me you don't deserve this; that partner is too right for you; this partner should be with somebody wealthier and more educated than you.

It was like I was setting myself up for a fall; I tried really hard, but soon as I nearly achieved my goal, everything would cease and go away. It's like I gave up just before the ending; imagine you went to a movie premiere, to perhaps get an award, but the award would be given to somebody else for lesser work; because you did not come through to the end, this is how I felt more than most times in my life. This has been going on for most of my life; it was like no matter what it did, it was never enough; one minute I would be ahead and the next behind.

The same thing happened in relationships; each time, I would meet somebody; something would go wrong. The spark and the connection will be there, and soon as things are moving along, everything will just end. And I would hear those words being uttered from me soon to be ex-partner regularly:

"you will find someone else,"

"it's not you; it's me,"

"We just want different things." - what happened to the opposite attract?

It's got so bad that I think once I actually even finished one of my ex-partner's sentences. It's like whatever I feared, became real. It was like I was living a nightmare of life, a never-ending night terror if you will.

After my divorce, I realized that this never-ending night terror was my life needed to either stop or I needed to wake up. So, I started exploring the phenomena behind my lousy luck. Because it got so bad that I attempted suicide; because I started to think that some people and family members would be better off without my bad luck in their life. After all, how much bad luck can one person take, I'm not to mention the heartache.

After my near-death experience, I woke up to life, some people say, "he died that day," while other people say; "he left, and some other being has taken over his body."

I dunno what happened after I passed out that day, but I must admit something changed.

And since then, I don't know whether it's my exploration at work or a higher power, realizing that I have been kicked to the floor one too many times.

But I have come along and realized that my symptoms of lousy luck are connected to disillusionment; I actually think disillusionment may explain the root cause of what I am experiencing.

Disillusionment is a philosophical term used to describe a feeling of disappointment of unsuccessful expectations. This is an exciting discovery for me because it finally sheds light on something that I have been feeling and couldn't quite put my finger on it to what was unhinging me from moving forward.

The disillusionment of something that was never going to happen for me because I lacked what a call, the 'in-between information.' The 'in-between information' is the variable that is needed to achieve success from point A to point B.

I seem to go from point A and then return to point A rather than point B.

It is confusing, I know!

Explanation

In layman's terms - my mind thinks too hard about the negative outcome and forgets to gather the information between point a and point b.

So, I may set off right, but, because the information is not there, my mind retracts me. It's like sending an email to address that doesn't exist; the email comes back to the sender.

I seem to set up okay but without a roadmap; and the information that I need to arrive on the other end.

Scientifically speaking, my mind collects information that is inconsequential to the task at hand. So, when the project is done, there isn't enough information to get to point B, so the variable returns from where it is come from, thus not finishing or achieving success.

Perhaps, in this case, a root cause is no longer needed; because it's not a case of pulling the problem out by its roots. It is more of a point trying to find a way to gather essential information rather than the inconsequential details being collected.

I will attempt to look at my past situations and, more importantly, investigate through scenarios to find out what has been going on. Moreover, to uncover the way my mind has been operating, perhaps this might be key to identifying why there is information missing!!

Scenario one:

I imagine that my partner is better than me because I know my faults,

The belief:

The thing was, I believed foolishly that my partner was going to leave me at any point in our relationship.

I lived like this for years, and each time we have a disagreement, for me, that time had arrived.

So,

I did what some people would have done. I grovelled and pleaded with my partner, and whatever my partner wanted, I gave my partner.

Variable of missing information:
1. I need to be aware of my new partner's faults.

2. I need to make it clear to my partner that we are in an equal relationship.

3. I need to explain to myself that I am good enough for my partner.

4. I need to explain to myself not to beg for anyone to stay in my life.

5. I need to believe if love and attention are not given freely, that it's not worth having.

6. I need to understand why I like my partner and find out it's not merely based on looks.

7. I need to find out how much my partner is invested in the relationship.

8. I need to learn to trust and love myself before I can do anything for anybody.

9. I need to not connect any form of happiness all good feelings to my partner whatsoever.

10. I need to learn never to beg anybody to stay in my life.

Scenario two:

My partner believed that better things and better people, better than me, we're out there.

The belief:

In the end, my partner left because my partner thought of one's self more important than us.

I remember my partner used to say to me the following:

"I could replace you within a click of a finger."

"I could've done so much better than you."

"why did I have to end up with you."

"All my cousin's sisters have wealthy educated men in their life, what's wrong with you."

"I have my eye on somebody, so I am thinking of leaving you."

"you were merely a means to an end."

After my partner left, it took me several years to come to terms with it.

Variable of missing information:

1. There is nobody better than anybody else, it is merely different.

2. If your partner is not happy with you, it is an issue for your partner to address.

3. No one can replace anybody, because no two people are alike, even twins have their differences.

4. Information regarding self-love, self-esteem, and confidence is missing.

5. Your partner has issues, which your partner needs to overcome by themselves.

6. Whatever doesn't work in your life, let it go.

7. Never try to bargain with your self-worth.

8. You weren't a right fit for each other perhaps

9. Perhaps you need somebody more alike.

10. Perhaps you need somebody that appreciates you and knows what they have.

Scenario three:

I became an erotomaniac,

The belief:

After I move forward without my partner, I became an erotomaniac; this, when I started to confuse the emotion of 'love,' whoever, I met I would be quick to say the words "I love you." Because I needed to fill an empty space inside.

So, my mindset was; to get in a new partner in my life, the sooner, the better. I just wanted someone to slot into my life, and some would move on from there. But the more I said those three magical words, the faster the women would run. In the end, I thought that every partner who looked at me, loved me, so, I pursued love like a quest uncontrollably until one day I just gave up.

This disillusionment of erotomaniac may unbalance a person as it may push a person's buttons. Because the person may think that people are in love with them based on a spark.

Variable of missing information:

1. Love is a tool; it is something that you do.
2. Love is a step in the process of being with another.
3. Love is not happiness.
4. A person can only love another as much as they love themselves.
5. There must be time to gather essential information outside your will to be with them.

6. There needs to be a balance between lusting after someone and living with someone.

7. Acknowledge another person becoming your loved one, rather than you are guiding them.

8. Follow your partner as much as they follow you.

9. There is more than one compatible mate, there is more than one love, there is more than one person for you.

10. Become happy before you can make somebody else delighted, happiness resides within one, not in somebody else.

I think I focus on, what I call, 'bettering the situation,' because I feel I am inadequate for the person that I am trying to woo. My mind is more focused on surprising the person rather than the moment that has presented itself. And because I'm concentrated in surprise in the person; I have in the past missed the 'moment' because, for some weird reason, my mind thinks a second one will present itself; perhaps this time next week, haha!

To make matters worse, after perhaps realizing that the 'moment' may not present itself again. I tend to have an array of embarrassing moments that surface to makeover romantic gestures.

Soon as my mind realizes that the moment has either disappeared or disappearing, my mind panics, and all of a sudden, my mind tries to adapt to the situation. By doing above and beyond, which, of course, can overwhelm some people. Not to mention by them, alcohol is in the mix too, so the mind is not thinking clearly either.

At the same time, for some odd reason, my mind is looking to create the exact moment, at a more convenient time. Perhaps looking for a way to postpone the 'moment,' I dunno!

Whereby my mind has time to plan events out to perfection, of course, there is no such thing as the perfect moment. So, my mind will try to over impress the person by overindulging in perhaps romance I dunno, or some good something that my mind perceives that person requires even though they haven't thought about it yet.

And in some extreme cases, perhaps I can say the three magic words, "I love you,"

Yes, I know!

The other person panics and runs,

So, I am glad that I have identified this disillusionment that I have been carrying around for most of my life. More importantly, understanding the variable of missing information from now on will be added before I set off. And I will make sure I pack a roadmap, if you will, to where I'm going. Funny enough, my forte is planning!

Below are some indicators to identify if you are experiencing disillusionment of erotomaniac behaviour.

The indicators

1. Irritable, inner anger – for not being attractive, can lead to severe pursuits of one's appearance.

2. Low-mood and perhaps Jealously

3.   Somatic – that some of us may have some sort of physical defect because some of us may find ourselves unable to embrace those imperfections that make us unique and different.

4.   Diverse disillusionment – has more than one disillusionment

The solution

1.   Self-worth knows what your self-worth is; knowing what you are worth can change people's preference of you dramatically. Some of us let people humour us and even sometimes let people dictate who and what some of us are. Because some people's perception of us seems to be better acknowledged by other people's input and opinions. Handing that kind of power to somebody else is basically admitting defeat to yourself. Knowing yourself who better than you can make that assumption.

2. Self-love, I have said this before, and I'll repeat it. Self-love means that you acknowledge your triumph. When you feel like you have accomplished enough, pat yourself on the back and appraise yourself for a job well done. Shake your own hand and high-five yourself. And if that isn't enough to look in the mirror and tell yourself that you're the right person and you have done a brilliant job. Admiring yourself in this manner simply means that you don't need others' opinions in your life. And more importantly, you love yourself. It might be an unorthodox way of doing something, and not to mention weird. But sometimes some of us need the appraisal of others. So why don't you give it to yourself rather than wait for other people to do just that? If somebody else appraises you, then that indeed is a +2.

My point is basically this, don't wait for other people to give you praise for your work. Once you have given a appraise to yourself, then the ball starts rolling. I used to hold my breath, seeking the first appraisal. However, when a critic would say something negative, the feeling inside would just bring me down to my knees. This way of appraising yourself no second negative opinion of somebody else can do just that, remember that above all else!

3. Unhinge your **FEARS**, because sometimes some of us can become unpredictable throughout emotions. Sometimes wants and needs can be confused, and sometimes some of us can take out our inner desires, on the wrong person from which sometimes some of us regret things that some of us do in the spur of the moment. Listen to your gut feeling and stop yourself from fearing different social situations. It is those uncomfortable situations that create room for fear. Face your fear before your fears face you.

4. Talk to a medical professional or a friend, talking is the best therapy as it helps us to realize the inner baggage that some of us burden ourselves with. Those embarrassing moments that some of us never share with the world until it's too late. Don't let the Pied Piper blow your trumpet for after the worst has passed. Blow the horn of fear earlier, let go of the past. By either writing things in a journal or telling someone about what has happened.

Tips!!

1. Self-worth, know what your self-worth is; knowing what you are worth can change people's preference of you dramatically. Some of us let people humour us and even sometimes let people dictate who and what some of us are. Because some people's perception of us seems to be better acknowledged by other people's input and opinions. Handing

that kind of power to somebody else is basically admitting defeat to yourself. Knowing yourself who better than you can make that assumption.

2.   Empty mindfulness issues of society in your mind, what people believe only may work for them, so meditate and clear out the emotional garbage of being alone before you're ready.

3.   Understand erotomaniac behaviour

4.   Unhinge your **FEARS**, because sometimes some of us can become unpredictable throughout emotions. Sometimes wants and

needs can be confused, and sometimes some of us can take out our inner desires, on the wrong person from which sometimes some of us regret things that some of us do in the spur of the moment. Listen to your gut feeling and stop yourself from fearing different social situations. It is those uncomfortable situations that create room for fear. Face your fear before your fears face you.

5. Simplify your life – start focusing on the simpler things and, more importantly, what works for you now. Rather than impress the people, impress yourself by making your life simple.

6. Meditate – listen to nothing, and nothing will control you; listen and refocus your mind and focus by blocking the world out by going into your own world within your mind.

7. Try something new and exciting, my suggestion try Yoga – there are 8 different types - try spiritual Yoga and experience something which may give you comfort in ways you haven't contemplated just yet.

My prayer

Bless me, my **GODS**, and Goddesses, this disillusionment has bought me to learn the real lesson of love. I realize now the difference in what I believed and what I should believe in. Thank you so much for this realization.

Chapter 8 – Suppression

Based on my past conversations, I believe I have ascertained unique perspectives surrounding the above issue. I Believe I have understood my situation a little better since the worst happened by analysing my last marriage. I did this by exploring critical conversations between my partner and me by examining the necessary details that lead up to the collapse of our marriage. I studied the subject above to some detail and used it to understand from this perspective to explore what faults occurred. From which I will explore why it happened and what I could have done to avoid it, and additionally, what I still can do to make sure history does not repeat itself. Some of us learn through experience, and some of us learn from mistakes created by us directly or indirectly. Nevertheless, after the collapse of something that was meant to last the full nine yards. I believe I needed to understand why and what went wrong, so I don't make the same mistake again.

So, here's what happened to me:

So, I could suppress anything that didn't fit into our lives because my partner wanted a better version of me.

For instance, I contained the need to have friends because my partner said: "your friends are a bad influence on you."

I think I should have stood up for myself from the very beginning and set boundaries.

I think this is the reason why my partner never could come to respect me. Because I let my partner control me. I gave my partner free rein to rule my life and make choices that influenced me outside of our relationship. Why would somebody respect someone they are protecting, as my partner became the protector, and I the protected?

Equality disappeared out of our relationship; I relied on my partner for everything. So, in many ways, my partner became the boss. Without knowing it, I handed over my power, freedom of choice, and the right to say no.

Whatever my partner wanted, I gave,

Whatever my partner didn't like about me, I changed,

Whatever I couldn't change, I suppressed.

At first, I didn't really mind, because everything was hunky-dory. I guess that was just all fun and games; until the game stopped and I realised I was the only one giving up things. I remember not liking one of my partners friends, so I asked my partner not to see this individual again. My partner replied, "you cannot tell me who I can and cannot see," that's when I realized that there were double standards in our relationship.

So, I figured, why should I suppress things when my partner won't! Of course, in the beginning, I stopped hiding small things, and I guess my partner just let things slide, but when we got to the big stuff. My partner actually requested me not to do certain things. That is when I realized I wasn't in a relationship; I was an emotional prison created by myself. And handed the key to my partner willingly.

So, from now, I started asserting invasive measures, whereby I would gain control for a short period. The argument period of our relationship had arrived, at the time when there was a power shift about. I wanted equality in a relationship, and my partner saw this as an aggressive takeover of my partners is power. More importantly, for some odd reason, my partner thought I was controlling. After my partner had been stopping me from doing things that I wanted, suddenly, I was getting accused of something my partner was doing to me.

I was really confused at this stage, forget about double standards. This was something entirely out of what I call the 'crazy book,' I mean, where was the middle ground, we went straight from my partner having the control to my partner accusing me of being controlling.

I thought 'me' having the reigns for a while may show my partner the error of one's ways. Instead, I was witnessing hostility because my partner did not want to relinquish my partner's control over me. From this period on either, I suppressed my issues, or I was being threatened with the relationship being over.

From this period, I needed to choose whether to stay in a steady relationship or be free alone. I had already become reliant on my partner for most things, so I could not detach, so I agreed to suppress whatever my partner wanted me to conceal. And of course, I had no say in where my partner went or with whom!

So, I suppressed things until one day, I got to the point where I couldn't hide any longer. So, with the fear of my partner leaving me, I started to release things that I had been suppressing for my partner. I had to do this behind my partner is back because otherwise, I was going to lose my partner.

The first thing I did, I made some friends, in a restaurant that I used to go to;

It was a high-class restaurant, where are used to go to eat, so nobody really lifted any eyebrows when I went there to meet friends and eat. My partner didn't suspect anything, so everything was okay for a while anyway.

So, while I was at this restaurant, I familiarized my new friends of what was going on at home. They seem to be shocked and told me nobody should be treated in that manner.

I explain to them of my neediness to be with my partner, they completely understood is that they were my friends. However, they also started to advise me of certain things that I needed to do to perhaps even things out. I wasn't looking for help, but I needed it really badly, my friends knew I needed it, I could see I needed it. So, after a while, I gave in, and my friends helped me understand my situation and little better, to say the least.

My friend's chats:

My friends said:
How much are you mesmerized by your partner?

My reply
I became infatuated and mesmerized with my partner because my partner is beautiful, and I like waking up beside my partner each day, knowing someone was there for me.

I realize this sounds like a cliché, but our relationship is like no other, as we connect in various ways effortlessly.

My friends said:

How much do you desire your partner?

My reply

Those who are fortunate to think in such a way; know that nothing else seems to matter.

My point is that we tend to give up anything for the person we desire the most.

My friends said:

Do you love your partner?

My reply

We were no different because we fell passionately in love with one another because we were together, even if it meant suppressing my individuality to please my partner.

My friends said:

Do you believe you are in the same relationship as your partner?

My reply

I guess there are two relationships taking shape occupying the same time frame.

My partner is in a relationship with the future me. And I am in a relationship with my partner in the present.

My friends said:

Are you happy, as you are the one who is suppressing your life?

My reply

We realized those imperfections that make us who we are, had either been suppressed or hidden away because we were trying so hard to please our future self's that some of us forgot about our present self's. The more some of us tried to be together, the further some of us drifted apart.

My friends said:

Are you happy?

My reply

I remember, we made each other miserable and pinched each other's enthusiasm.

My friends said:

Do you love your partner?

My reply

Yes, but of course,

My friends said:

What do you love about your partner?

My reply

My partner... yes, I love my partner, why wouldn't I live my partner... I love everything about my partner.

That's when I realized, things are over, I didn't want to admit it.

I guess we left each other empty, uncompleted with delusions of being with the perfect partner, from which I look back and realize why some people believe it's best to have loved and lost rather than never loved.

My friends said:

Would I suppress again,

My reply:

'No, never again.'

My friends said:

Why?

My reply:

Because it has taken nearly a while to find who I am, I got buried under all of my partner's expectations, and I lost my own individuality in the process.

My friends said:

Talks us through your experience.

My reply:

Suppression starts with hiding small imperfections about one's self, which for me comprised of:

- Trying to please someone overly.
- Suppressing my thoughts and mindset to make room for my partner's way of thinking.
- Changed my thinking patterns, so I could think like my partner.
- Became obsessive over my partner – which lead to overprotection issues.
- I suppressed my need to think about the girl before my partner.
- I buried terrible habits.
- I deleted the need to have friends.
- My fashion sense changed because I stifled who I was.

- I suppressed socializing and networking because my partner thought I may bump into old acquaintances.

The list is endless,

My friends said:

How could you advise someone if somebody was being suppressed?

My reply:

You can start to understand your individuality and recognize why you feel like your thoughts are conflicted and why views don't make sense anymore.

Also, you may want to read this:

The indicators

1. Giving up on dreams.

2. Looking into an uncertain future with beliefs of not doing something.

3. Fear of being alone.

4. Looking for happiness in my partner's dreams.

5. Holding back for a perfect time.

6. Becoming something you are not.

The solution

1.   Complete all goals without suppressing them. No matter what, never hide your plans for nobody. Never tried to impress somebody by following their path; remember when that moment wears off, you will be the person left with the suppressed goals.

2.   Trust in the higher power and the universe – and let things shape naturally if something doesn't come naturally, then there is no point in having it. Remember to grow. The flowers never struggled to bloom, they just bloom. Tree's don't get tired of standing upright, they just stand there for hundreds of years. Because that is the natural order of things. If you believe in the words "when it will be it will be," that is a natural way, the natural order of things will happen.

Otherwise, some of us run the risk of being in the wrong place at the wrong time. I believe it usually comes under the term 'bad timing.' The universe will put us in the right place at the right time. So for now, do what you need to do without worrying about what the plan for you is.

3.   Loneliness. Some of us are only ever lonely when some of us think some of us are alone; because each time some of us tend to focus on loneliness, the universe gives us just that. Rather than focus on something that you don't want. Focus on being with people without them, and soon the universe will put people in your path because that is what you have asked for. Of course, some critics may or may not believe in a higher power or the universe, but this is not a fact for them to argue, this is merely a theory with cosmic powers attached to it. Just believe and walk your path; the rest will unfold eventually. Know this. Some of us come from nothing, and some of us go with nothing. So perhaps the universe has answers that some of us know not of. Or maybe it's just a game of the gods. Keep moving forward because there's nothing behind.

4.   Be true to yourself because no one else will - stop trying to be somebody else or worse trying to mimic somebody else's life.

We all have the destiny to follow, so follow your future and stop focusing on other people's lives unless it has some implications for your life.

Sometimes some of us just want to be somebody else; of course, there is nothing wrong with that. However, remember to advance to your next level of change without following other people.

Because the chances are you may swerve of your own path and end up lost on somebody else's way.

Every now and again, some of us get signs posted in our lives. To guide us to the right places and at the right time.

Stay on your path of life, and those who are supposed to be there will remain. And those who have played a part in your life will predominately wander off.

Think about the analogy of a motorway or a freeway. Many turns come off and on every now and again. Some people get along, and some people get out; the highway or freeway is your life.

The junctions that come on and off your motorway or freeway represent people that come into your life. And the people that wander out of your life.

There is no set time for this to happen; it is merely that they have reached the end of the journey with you on your journey.

Keep driving forward because more people will join your life journey, stop looking at your rear-view mirror. Or you would run the risk of not noticing who gets on at what junction.

Tips!!

1. Stop procrastinating

2. Grow into the newer version of yourself

3. Trust in the **GODS**, as those who leave things in **GODS** hands, then **GODS** hand will be in everything

4. Don't wait, the perfect time is now

My prayer

Dear GODS, and Goddesses,

I leave everything in your hands.

Help me with your power,

as I am ready for my next chance at love and life.

Chapter 9 – The emotional flood gates

Based on my past conversations, I believe I have ascertained unique perspectives surrounding the above issue. I Believe I have understood my situation a little better since the worst happened by analysing my last marriage. I did this by exploring critical conversations between my partner and me by examining the necessary details that lead up to the collapse of our marriage. I studied the subject above to some detail and used it to understand from this perspective to explore what faults occurred. From which I will explore why it happened and what I could have done to avoid it, and additionally, what I still can do to make sure history does not repeat itself. Some of us learn through experience, and some of us learn from mistakes created by us directly or indirectly. Nevertheless, after the collapse of something that was meant to last the full nine yards. I believe I needed to understand why and what went wrong, so I don't make the same mistake again.

So, here's what happened to me:

As far back as I can remember, I was always on a rebound of some sort.

When I met my partner, I had just lost a partner that I loved dearly. I was looking for someone to make me whole.

So, when I met my partner, a world of emotions came to the forefront of what was going to be a seven-year train wreck.

Her compassion and support were phenomenal; I had never witnessed anything like it.

So, I started relying on that incredible support, which soon turned into infatuation because I never had someone care for me so profoundly. I became reliant on my partner's love and support.

My emotional flood gates opened, and I think it overwhelmed her. `I was a train wreck, and my partner was picking up the pieces from the last relationship that I was in.

I guess the timing was off or something, I was a what I call a pasteurizer, who went from partner to partner, each time pleasing the next one.

The thing with pleasing people; it leads one to adopt other people's mindsets, from which in some cases, one can lose their individuality in the process. Sometimes being around others, we sometimes start to mimic other people's actions, soon we find ourselves encompassed in other people's mindsets through repetitive indirect learning. Basically, when you start hanging around with somebody too much. Some of us tend to pick up some more traits that identify them through us. If this is too often enough, sometimes we can forget who we are and become someone entirely different.

In my case, I took it a step further; I actually learned other people's traits, because I thought I could become like them. Because I only ever saw that highlights of their and from this, I gathered that their life was better than my own. So, I started hanging with people that had Boundary. Issues moral issues. Anti-destructive behavioural issues. Through which I became an ego-eccentric person who thought of nothing other than the people I looked up to.

I lost myself a while ago; I simply mimicked too many people, to say the least, and somewhere in there, I lost my personality, individuality,

Independence, and my own unique character. I never had any friends growing up, so I didn't know how to communicate with people until later years. And well I would date somebody I would let them control me advertently because I was taught that happiness comes when one is with their other half. Being that there was no public access to the Internet at the time. So, whatever people in general said, we just went along with it.

My partner was going to unravel layers of my different personalities, and people-pleasing masks without knowing it. The thing was; I was a mess; I had been taken advantage of many a time; to me, users and abusers work common day folk. When my partner saw me, I had similarities to my partner's father and brother. Who Both had similar emotional baggage like me? I think this one of the reasons why my partner was drawn to me. Sometimes what we record in our minds growing up tends to dictate our lives in the present somewhat. Without acknowledging how we are proceeding; we tend to sometimes mimic what we have learned in the past by copying it into the present by picking the people that we are most comfortable with. Regardless of whether people good or bad.

God bless my partner, as my partner tried more so than anyone else, however, I needed professional help, and at the time, I didn't want to fix myself because I couldn't see a problem.

I was a wrong person; happy go lucky person with the knack to get into trouble because I made snap judgments, which lead me down dark paths.

So,

You can imagine the neediness that came from that!

It was far more than my partner could handle, and with the added bonus of childhood issues; and the ever-growing list of disorders, learning difficulties, mental health issues, self-destructive patterns, paranoia, insecurity, and many other issues and problems. Things looked bleak to start with.

Anyway,

I remember this one-time coming home 'drunk as a skunk' and barely able to climb into bed; my partner would unclothe me while arousing me.

My partner liked drunk intimacy as my partner would take charge; my partner would never let that be known; however, according to my partner, "it was the fastest way to get me asleep."

After hearing that, I must say I did sometimes play along; sometimes, when I wasn't really too drunk, I would pretend that I was more intoxicated than I was, knowing full well my partner would have to put-out to put me into bed.

Haha!

That's when I saw how much my partner liked being on top and in charge.

I looked up to my partner as my problem fixer and, more importantly, someone I could turn to when I needed someone to talk too, someone who could support me through anything I dished out,

I see it now, I was an attention seeker, and the more my partner helped me, the more I would rely on my partner.

From which, I became dependent on my partner for everything; thus, the neediness just grew out of control; it was like an addiction, the more my partner put up with me, the more I burdened my partner with my issues. Until one day, when my partner simply walked out of my life.

Some of us never realize how dependent some of us can be and how much emotional baggage we sometimes carry into a relationship. Without knowing what some of us are doing until it is too late.

Because some of us tend to hide our emotional baggage. Under the infatuation of being with someone.

Some of us may hide our imperfections because some of us are ashamed of them. But this brings more issues as you offload your emotional baggage at a later date.

Some of us have more emotional baggage than others and personal issues.

Most of us have emotional issues, especially when we age, as life takes its twists and turns through the loopholes of life. Weekend to overshadow and overwhelm the person that closest to us. It is difficult not to do this because then we can be accused of being detached from our emotions. This is a tricky area because we need to realize how much the floodgates need to open. And out what time of the relationship. The problem lies when people sometimes do not tell their partner everything. In fear of that, they tend to divulge too much, which tends to overwhelm some people.

Obviously, within my story, there were times when I supported my partner as well. Still, I thought I should give my partner some applause for something that my partner has done in our relationship, which is truly memorable. It also makes it easier to explain the phenomena behind the floodgates of emotions.

Now for my exploration, I have discovered a unique way to Open the floodgates without too much flowing out.

Below there are some ways that you can tactfully explain in a nutshell to your partner about the emotional baggage that you carry behind your floodgates. If you open your front gate slowly and now, only a stream will flow out of controlled emotional baggage problems and issues; rather than an ocean of overwhelming matters or complications.

1. Focus on less is more because people want to know everything, but they want to know it in a nutshell.

2. Try grouping things together, one of the easiest ways of doing this is to explain events in your life chronologically. The age grouping is outstanding because you know where you left off, and you know what else is left to tell your partner.

3. Never explain in detail, try and keep it short and sweet (**KISS**). Too much detail tends to trigger far too many emotions and something that you're not ready to tell the person may drop out at the wrong time. So be warned on that!

4. Try and place emotions in individual groups and try to detach from connecting one issue to another.

5. Take regular breaks when divulging personal information; this is done by gaining some insight from whoever you're explaining this to. Pretend you're playing table tennis, you talk about emotion and then hit the ball over to the other side for some advice. The more you involve the other person, the less likely you are too overwhelming them.

6. Practice makes perfect, sit somewhere quiet, and talk to yourself. Record yourself and then playback to see what you're about to divulge to your partner.

7.   Get a diary, this is probably an excellent way of doing things. Because you can get everything out of your head, and you can decide in what context everything comes out.

8.   If there is something in your past that you do not want to discuss or mention to your partner, I would recommend deep-rooted meditation. It will clear out anything and everything. (And prevent things coming out when you're intoxicated).

9.   Explain things as you would want to hear them, sometimes we need to sugar-coat things because women regret the guys that they have slept with. And the guys regret the women they didn't sleep with. So sometimes it is best to humourize any topics surrounding that.

10. No matter how you feel, your other half is not your best friend; they are there to support you and primarily have intimate relations with you. Don't confuse my best friends' heart to heart with that over future partners' emotional flood gate opening.

11. Know what you're saying even when you are in an erratic mode.

Mistakes

1. Never talk to your partner's family before you speak to them.

2. Never talk to your partner's friends before you talk to your partner.

3. Never speak to your own friends about the pre-conversation that you're going to have with your partner. As this causes problems in the future, in a nutshell, we don't always get along with people; don't give people leverage against you.

4. Never be in a rush to explain everything in one go.

5. Never lie outright, if you need to cover something up, again meditate.

6. Remember, life partners, are not best friends. If you believe this, then you going to do one of two things – you're either going to tell them too much, and they may use that against you at a later date. Or are you going to give them a get out of jail card. Remember being with a partner is an everyday investment. Don't set yourself for a fall, Best

friends with partners tend to sometimes result as best friends only in the end.

There is no such thing as being too needy; neither is there much research surrounding dependability, unless you're talking about a child with a parent, of course, that is a different matter entirely. We tend to have problems dealing with emotional baggage issues, some of us tend to divulge too much information too quickly. Because we find a connection with someone and all of a sudden, we overload the voltage and instead of a spark we get a very loud bang. So, from this period on the separation process begins, if you catch my drift. I have actually lived through this and the information above is based on my personal experience, perhaps my misfortunes can benefit somebody else in understanding what to do and when to do it. Because in the day and age that we live in, it is difficult to find the 'one' so rather than make a boo-boo of the situation, treading lightly and slowly is the order of the day.

There are indicators below to see if you have this issue because sometimes, we don't realize what some of us are doing wrong until it's too late.

Maybe this is the information that made all the difference in your future endeavours, I dunno!

But it can't hurt!

The indicators

1. Avoiding arguments, leave the room if necessary.

2. Fear – we all have this, we all need this, it keeps us safe from the uncertainties of the unfamiliar situations, learn to embrace it rather than fear it.

3. Living in the shadow of another – why live in the shadows, then you have a life to lead. Don't confuse love lost with stupidity. Love is never lost because it is something one performs, not fails. It is merely a tool, not an emotion or a part of you.

4. Trying to control the future – nothing is certain, everything is possible, let go of something you cannot stop and wait for the future that hasn't come to past yet.

The solution

1. Don't be too agreeable, but at the same time, agree to disagree.

2. Please don't change your plans to fit someone into them; think what is best for me, and then add the person to your goals. Of course, this works both ways.

3. Think forward, rather than look back at what's gone. Of course, this is after one separate. Sometimes moving on can be daunting.

4. Stop being needy and resolve co-dependency issues. Stand up on your own two feet and start becoming self-efficient.

5. Identify needy people and keep them at arm's length; recognize this quickly and start to educate people rather than push them away, perhaps hand them a copy of this book.

6. Stop overthinking and start doing; because life is short and the time to think is the last thing at night when some of us take stock of what some of us have.

Tips!!

1. Stop relying on people

2. Become self-efficient

3. Question other motives

4. Believe your inner critic

5. Become my own best friend

6. Be open-minded

7. Stop people-pleasing

8. Let others give advice

9. Meditate

My prayer

Bless me, heavenly fathers and mothers, I have come so far, and the road behind me is considerably longer than the road ahead in terms of competing my ordeals, please give me the chance to be with another life partner. I have learned the lesson well and will not be making such mistakes again.

Chapter 10 – Letting go

Based on my past conversations, I believe I have ascertained unique perspectives surrounding the above issue. I Believe I have understood my situation a little better since the worst happened by analysing my last marriage. I did this by exploring critical conversations between my partner and me by examining the necessary details that lead up to the collapse of our marriage. I studied the subject above to some detail and used it to understand from this perspective to explore what faults occurred. From which I will explore why it happened and what I could have done to avoid it, and additionally, what I still can do to make sure history does not repeat itself. Some of us learn through experience, and some of us learn from mistakes created by us directly or indirectly. Nevertheless, after the collapse of something that was meant to last the full nine yards. I believe I needed to understand why and what went wrong, so I don't make the same mistake again.

So, here's what happened to me:

I distinctly remember during the last couple of years as our relationship drew to an end, as I frantically tried to reconnect with my partner on some level to salvage something. I guess I wasn't ready to let go just then!

I could see that we were heading in the way of the dodo. But it seems pointless; whatever I tried; I vividly recall my partner not wanting to re-establish a connection with me. I just wanted things back to what they use to be like, I guess!

My partner would corroborate anything I said or did with someone else and then either dismiss my thought-out ideas or reject my romantic jesters and advances. It was like someone was whispering in my partner's ear. I guess I was feeling left out! It just would have been nice if my partner confided in me. That's all.

From this point, it seemed pointless,

I was nobody special, and it seemed I wasn't going anywhere fast. And I think my partner could see that. The more I tried to please my partner, the more I failed in life; I believe in the end, my partner just saw a person that's wasn't going to amount to anything, I guess!

I think we gave up on each other and got to the point where we knew it was all over but were too pig-headed to admit it.

My partner confiding in other people didn't help the situation much. in fact, the thoughts that we're circulating in my mind; "my partners got someone of the side; is my partner cheating on me."

On the other hand, I started to become overzealous and started advancing with overly dreamy jesters that I had previously not had time for. I dunno!

I had a mindset of an earlier happy time, and my partner just became distant. Late nights turned into overnight stays. Often, my partner would lie and go somewhere and then say, "I wasn't there, don't know what you are talking about." It got unreal so-fast, I guess! I mean, my partner would lie to the entire family whenever my partner saw fit. So, I think my partner became a compulsive liar in the end.

I think my partner was cheating on me, I had no proof, but my partner was seen out and about shopping with other partners. I remember some things didn't add up, such as money missing from bank accounts and my jewellery on occasion disappearing. What reaffirmed my suspicions each time was little things like I remember once in bed when we were making love, there was something different about the last few times we were together. It was like my partner was face fucking me. I got the distinct impression that my partner was imagining someone else's face on my body and making love to that person rather than me.

I stayed quiet because I figured if my partner wanted to go, then my partner will go. After all, I wasn't in my partner's league so, perhaps it was that time. Maybe our day in the sun had come to an end.

Self-destructive patterns emerge, and some of us adapt our lifestyle to accommodate this new change of circumstance. A place where dreams go to die, a place deep inside where all the hopes seem hopeless, as we accept that feeling of insecurity and uncertainty of moving on. So, we adapt ourselves in filling that void deep inside by overeating whatever my desire. Because we feel no one may care about the few extra pounds. Because the thing called 'love' no longer plays a part in my life. What once was a whole embodiment of love; is now just a broken half shell of a person; left to wallow in self-pity.

It is these times some of us really take stock of what we really want out of life. I blamed my partner for everything, as my partner probably blamed me too.

However, rather than point fingers and make a bad situation into a worse one. Sometimes we just need to recharge and re-find ourselves again. It was easy for my partner to move on, so one would like to think. But is it ever; I have to believe deep inside my partner does miss me. Since it is that kind of thinking which is pulling me through this.

One last branch which I am clinging on too that is making me functions whole again.

Twist – in this chapter to explain the above in another way of thinking!

It took seven years to heal,

The ironic thing is that some of us were together from start to finish for seven years.

Then the mirror broke.

The curse was unleashed by unintentionally breaking a mirror; this is commonly known as the curse of the broken mirror. If you break a mirror, an evil of seven years, bad luck will be unleashed on the person responsible.

It is thought, that soon as the mirror breaks, cracks or shatters. All the problems that mirror has seen are unleashed to the person responsible for opening the rift between the mirrored world that is on the other side of the mirror.

So, began our 7 years of bad luck, but who broke the mirror indeed is the question?

Well, whatever helps really, because in the end we need closure, and if it helps to close the pas by believing in a curse, then I guess there is nothing wrong with that. I needed to think that something else was a mist! After all, we are all human, and moving on sometimes requires one to look for an answer outside of human perception and understanding. I guess it just makes life liveable again.

I think about my partner sometimes, as my mind wanders to the far reaches of the universe. Because I have those flashbacks of a better time, from which I struggle to let go.

Letting go is never easy. Nonetheless, it's happened; the way I think about it is that we will meet again, or at least bump into one another again.

For now, I realize that if we do cross paths again, do I want my partner to see me as a pathetic mess or a success?

It may be a lonely journey for a while but, I see this as the training part of my life, leading up to show my partner that I wasn't a failure, and if my partner had just a little more faith, we could have been happier together perhaps!

The journey will be lonesome, but hey, on the way to impressing my ex-partner, I may bump into my future partner. That in itself gets me out of bed and transpires me to do better each day.

Sometimes being in a weird competition with your ex-partner can give one that pushes that we need to become something we were always meant to be. I believe something is at work, a higher power if you will because when something pressures are taken from us, it sometimes is replaced with something better. And having that belief makes me function, as this insight gives rise to my shattered heart to become whole again. Knowing that my happy ever after is still out there.

My story doesn't end here!

<u>The indicators</u>

1. Failing to take action START

2. Harbouring self-defeat thoughts STOP

3. Forced incompetence – feeling unintelligent STOP

4. Not taking responsibility START

5. Placing blame STOP

6. Overthinking STOP

7. Overindulging STOP

8. Listening to strangers for advice STOP

9. Sabotaging my own mind with destructive thought patterns STOP

The solution

1. Identify triggers START

2. Let go of fear START

3. Listen to the inner child and gut feelings START

4. Communicate with one another START

5. Re-enactment of happier times START

6. Meditate START

7. Travel and do something new START

8. Mindfulness meditations to clear the emotional baggage that some of us have inside. START

9. Take a break and give each other space, START

Tips!!

1. Physical and mental neglect focus on you.

2. Educate yourself, as knowledge is the key to the world.

3. Get professional help, a different inside from a different perspective.

4. Under and overeating - consume a balanced diet.

5. Take control of the life you have and live it to the best of your ability.

6. Choose to make your experience better after you read this book. Make that promise to yourself, and things will start to materialize out of nowhere.

Secret Tip!!

Compile 4 lists about what you do not want in your life!

1. Write a list of all your problems.
2. Write a list of all the people who have done wrong by you.
3. Write a list of all the bad situations you were in.
4. Write a list of all the negative things in your life.

And then

Compile another 4 lists about what you do want in your life!

1. Write a list of all the people that care about you.
2. Write a list of all who have been there for you.
3. Write a list of all the beautiful places you have been to.
4. Write a list of all the real situations in your life.

Build a fire, doesn't have to be big, a small pot lined with foil will suffice.

Add the following ingredients:

1. Lavender plant or oil
2. Sage
3. Rosemary
4. Thyme
5. Bay leaves
6. Piece of blank white paper

Light the fire and place the lists with all the things you do not want into it. And then think about them for the last time.

Then!

Do the same with all the things you do want in your life!

And from this process, the healing process starts, and the universe hears your voice.

Things will start to look brighter.

My prayer

Bless me, dear Gods, Goddesses, Angels, and the universe I have come so far, and I now realize the true meaning of relationships, I have learned this lesson and will keep improving. Thank you for showing me a different way. 🙏

Chapter 11 – The Insecurities manipulation through submission

Based on my past conversations, I believe I have ascertained unique perspectives surrounding the above issue. I Believe I have understood my situation a little better since the worst happened by analysing my last marriage. I did this by exploring critical conversations between my partner and me by examining the necessary details that lead up to the collapse of our marriage. I studied the subject above to some detail and used it to understand from this perspective to explore what faults occurred. From which I will explore why it happened and what I could have done to avoid it, and additionally, what I still can do to make sure history does not repeat itself. Some of us learn through experience, and some of us learn from mistakes created by us directly or indirectly. Nevertheless, after the collapse of something that was meant to last the full nine yards. I believe I needed to understand why and what went wrong, so I don't make the same mistake again.

So, here's what happened to me:

Sometimes some of us take our emotional baggage into our relationships, which is fine, nothing wrong with that. But, there's those of us who never come to terms with our past. And in turn, end up punishing the new relationship each time something from the past bear's similarity to a present situation. I did just that; I blamed myself for years, but the blame isn't going to heal you; understanding what you are doing and coming to terms with the past is the key.

This book is merely an insight for you to recognize you may have insecure issues; from this, you can identify what you should and should not do. It is that simple, the rest a counsellor can guide you, because face it, the rest is a story which ends by you accepting the past and closing the door to the past and moving on. But before you do move on, forgive the past, or you run the risk of living in it until you face it.

This is what I did!!

Part one: don't be me, learn from my insecurities' - my past and what happened to me.

My insecurities' - I had a rather tough childhood that comprised of being bullied and pushed about by several people. And not to mention growing up in a lonely, weird way on account of my brother is ten years older. My weirdness comprises of doing things that were always outside the society's boundaries because my brother was in a gang in the '80s who would introduce me to unsavoury characters who would push me about behind my brothers back.

I would be hurt and embarrassed anytime my brother had his friends around; I would be locked under the stairs until I conformed to my brothers and his friend's way of thinking. I was obligated to remove my trousers anytime my brother wanted a laugh with his mates, under duress, and in fear of the punishment I did as they asked as my so-called-brother took photos of my privates and later put them on display. I guess I was lucky there were no social media at the time, I was 6 years old, and was ashamed of myself when people pointed at me and laughed; not to mention they said: "it's your fault for apparently letting him take pictures." So, as time passed and I grew up, I started to see life through the eyes of a scared child. I would get into trouble because; I didn't know any other way to get attention. I was under the impression people would never believe me if I told the truth because I was informed by my brother's mates that if I ever told a soul, they would deny it and show everyone the pictures, informing people that I posed for them.

So, scarred for life,

Part two: so, when I met my partner, my insecurities manifested into conformity and regular practice over her.

I started to overprotect my partner due to insecurity issues and paranoia of losing her in some way. Not to mention, I knew my partner was out of my league. So, in my mind, it wasn't a case of 'if' my partner would leave, it was a case of 'when.'

And guess what! My fears came to light.

I turned into her' bodyguard.'

We never went out in the night anywhere, because I thought people would attack us from the shadows.

I would not let my partner go out alone anywhere and would start an argument if I heard otherwise. At some stage, I think in many ways, I may have treated my partner like one would do their possessions.

What's worse,

She came from a strict family, and boyfriends were not allowed. This fear just made me into an emotional wreck, so I became paranoid about potential threats that could happen. Because of our fear of getting caught by my partner's family, I started an undercover mission, this comprised me taking weird, strange measures for us to be together. It was like we were on a secret mission; it was her and me against the world.

I remember soon as my partner would arrive by train, I would have a car waiting for my partner to be picked up and bought it for my place.

Each time my partner visited, it was like a prised military operation; it became our thing, the sneaking around was thrilling, exciting, and enjoyable, living in a James Bond-like film at the beginning. Just like any other relationship, it was something new, and some of us just went with the flow. Not to mention the intimacy was out of this world.

It worked then because I was getting a booty call regularly; it was beautiful at first until we realized everything we did was based mainly in the bedroom.

My partner wanted to be taken out, wined, & dined, I guess we needed time away from the bedroom. However, my partner's family was always on the prowl. The father was a drunk, so pubs were out of the question. The younger sister was a party animal like me, so clubs and nightlife were tricky. And not to mention the older sister & brother who worked near a town, so daytime was risky too. And my partner's mother always had a suspicious mind and informed all of my partner's relatives to keep an eye out if they saw my partner anywhere.

I needed to go out and breathe and be with my friends, and my partner hated me meeting my friends because my partner was under the impression that all we did was drink and party. My partner wasn't wrong, as we were binged drinkers and loved to party. Laughing out loud (Lol).

So, I went out and got drunk, sometimes I only had a couple of hours, so, if I didn't drink fast, then I wouldn't get drunk, so it was fortunate I was a binged drinker.

Sometimes, we would go out on occasions, such as valentine's day, but only if a security detail was available. And I would develop eyes at the back of my head, in case we were spotted. Not to mention worried for both of us. In terms of my partner getting in trouble and me losing my partner earlier than expected.

I think my partner felt like a prisoner to some degree,

I thought I was protecting my partner from adversaries that we hadn't encountered yet. I became overprotected of my partner and restricted her movements. I remember this one time my partner said a student at the university my partner was attending was bothering my partner, as my partner refused the person advances, as the person wasn't taking no for an answer.

Part three, insecurities learning the art of manipulation through submission.

So,

I went to see this person and wanted to really harm him, but I was afraid of my own shadow and afraid of a comeback when I wasn't around. Hence, I devised a cunning plan by antagonizing the person through the art of manipulation. I gave the person an option; to apologize, the minders were going to embarrass the person ostensibly in an unscrupulous manner. Since I remember a similar thing done to me, and I remembered the embarrassment and the ridicule that followed with it.

I informed the person, 'if I ever heard of this person behaving in this manner again, then the punishment would go ahead without warning.

So, the person agreed, and they never bothered my partner, nor any one's else's a partner for that matter ever again.

So, that day,

I gained power over people and realized how I could manipulate them into submission.

This was great for me, but not so great for my partner because soon, I started to influence my partner into submission without knowing. For example, if my partner wanted to do something, I would make it, my partners choose not to do it. That way, I was protecting my partner from predators like myself.

Be assured,

I felt ashamed, but I didn't realize what I was doing; after all, there was no internet to guide us.

She was very naïve and innocent, and my partner wasn't aware of the wolfs of society; but the fact was, what I didn't know then, I was a wolf too.

My views of the world where simple back then; a world of con artists to get my partner into bed.

Because I could see it happening, after all, I got my partner into bed quite quickly, so I just thought perhaps my partner may be coerced into it somehow. After all, my partner had fantasies about being with other partners. Mainly because I was my partner first, and I had had several ex-partners. So, I think my partner felt it should have been equal rather than me having more experience than her.

Part four: enforcing my insecurities over my partner

I would hear stories of girls being drugged and then taken advantage of, and rather than discuss this with her. I belittled my partner and told my partner what my partner could and could not do.

I was a late bloomer in the sense of having a confident mindset. So, my insecurities became my partner's insecurities, and eventually, this manifested into paranoia for me.

As for my partner, my partner grew up.

I remained a control freak; it wasn't till I educated myself, I learned what I had become, but unfortunately, my partner was long gone by then.

I just loved my partner too much to let anything wrong happen to her. Instead, I became a paranoid lunatic that had emotional issues and deep-rooted child abuse issues to deal with, which were being used as a defence mechanism, according to my therapist. I became this broken individual who learned very slowly because I was dyslexic, according to my counsellor.

Part five: recognizing deep-rooted disorders that were suppressed deep inside

Each time my partner would threaten to leave me, this broken person would appear and beg my partner to stay. And being the person, my partner was, my partner just gave in, and it just got worse each time. We broke up a fair few times, and I would call my partner back each and every time until I didn't, or my partner had enough.

Part six: destructive patterning through submission of insecurities

It wasn't until later, I discovered I was a neurotic pessimist that was displaying obsessive-compulsive disorder syndrome (OCD) symptoms with notably high anxiety issues, and borderline personality disorder (BPD) patterned behaviour. Until these issues were diagnosed, my relationships didn't go so well, according to the General hospital secondary care unit.

This is why I believe a person should evolve before seeking out a potential partner, or you run the risk of hurting many people and having a multitude of ex-partners in your path of destruction.

I have great respect for women, and can't believe who I was,

the plot deepens,

I just need to get this message to any partners that are currently doing this.

Because it is not your partner, it is you.

Looking back, I have lived in resentment for nearly a decade, and if I could turn the clock back, I would, but I can't, well not in a conventional way.

But I can make sure others learn from my mistakes.

The indicators

1.

Trimming perfectionism - Do you try to perfect things? Do you work too hard to make mistakes? Do you focus on appearances more? Do you like putting people in their place? Then you have a problem.

2. Do you point out people's imperfections and flaws? Do you think it is a perfect world? Do you think you can change someone? Do you think you can walk someone else path better for them? Then you have a problem.

3. Are you a people pleaser? Do you place more emphasis on other's opinions above your own? Do you find yourself helping others overly? Do you feel the need to go that extra mile to help people? Then you have a problem.

4. Blaming others for your issues and problems? Do you think others are to blame for your problems? Do you think people are more

focussed on their lives? Do you think people should make time for you as you do for them? Then you have a problem.

5. Do you feel helpless? Do you want people to care about you overly? Do you think some people make you a priority? Do you like attention too? Do you seek attention from others overly? Then you have a problem.

6. High anxiety – Do you feel suffocated at times? Do you feel anxious? Do you feel like the world is closing around you? Do you contact like some people are out to hurt you? Then you have a problem. For this one, please seek medical advice.

7. Do you overly try to find like-minded people? Do you think people do not like you? Do you think friends are hard to come by? Do you think you do not deserve friends? Then you have a problem.

8. Are you a boaster - bragger person? Do you overly say things that you want? Do you advertise your work before it is finished? Do you have unrealistic goals? Do you think people are there to serve you? Then you have a problem.

9. Do you criticize frequently? Are you being moaner? Do you see the fault in everything? Do you hold someone responsible for your actions? Do you think there is someone to blame every time? Then you have a problem.

When some of us feel insecure, some of us hesitate when some of us trust ourselves, this leads to us taking decisive action to get to a desirable outcome. Some of us tend not to take proactive action, and this leads us to daunt ourselves, and some of us also tend to judge ourselves harshly and start to blame our actions on others to prevent others from observing our imperfections. From which some of us can use people to further boost our expectations of ourselves in front of others. This primarily builds a false realization of one's own self-esteem, because soon as some of us run out of victims, the self-esteem runs out too alone with others trusting us.

The solution

1. Take stock of your values and start keeping a journal to keep your accounts in order. Just as you would with your finances, keep things balanced. Make lists of your likes and dislikes and start changing the dislikes into equivalents as you invest in yourself.

2. Stop people-pleasing and start pleasing yourself. Relax more and delegate tasks.

3. Start taking responsibility for your own actions; own yourselves by owning up to whatever you haven't been doing. Take a deep dive into your affairs and see if there's anything that needs altering.

4. Build your self-esteem up; stand up for yourself. Strengthen your inner child and unleash the gut feeling. Because only you can fix yourself. Go to a retreat and become one with nature and repair your confidence by knowing yourself properly.

5. Build a trust circle, delete all your contacts from your phone and sit back and see who contacts you. The first five people in the early five days are your inner circle. The second five days after that become your outer circle. The rest are people who say they care, not people who do. Know the difference!

6. Become humble and noble, start looking for the positive in the negative. And then begin to use things and love people. Because face it, some of us use people and love materialistic things.

7. Stop obsessing over what's no longer serves you; whatever you are holding onto, let go, whatever's holding you back, let go; whatever's, hurting you, let go. It is only you who is holding on to your troubles.

8.

Unburden yourself; look into a child's eyes and see what is there. View the world through a child's mind; become the child. As your inner child surfaces, watch the knots untangle.

9.

Understand your imperfections; become you again; come out of under what seems like a mountain of other people's perceptions of you.

Tips!!

1.

Controlling the future – can't stop an ever-changing end.

2. Fearful of losing my partner – lost her, be the man I want to be before the next girl arrives into my life

3. Except who I am – change into me, not the person I think my partner will want to be with

4. Talk it out with professionals

5.

Overcome my OCD

6.

Overcome my PBD

7. Get my paranoia into check

8. Bring down my anxiety level from high to low

9. Stop being a doormat for all to walk over.

It's not about what's gone, it's about the lesson if it was learned. Because the next person will be looking for equality, and if you cannot give that, you're not ready to step out of the workshop of life. Think about a car you are fixing up, get it to a standard, and then take it for a test drive.

My prayer

Bless me, GOD, / higher power, as I have abused my ability as a man and became the destruction of my own demise, please forgive, and please let me become a righteous and respectful man.

Chapter 12 – From worrier to warrior

Based on my past conversations, I believe I have ascertained unique perspectives surrounding the above issue. I Believe I have understood my situation a little better since the worst happened by analysing my last marriage. I did this by exploring critical conversations between my partner and me by examining the necessary details that lead up to the collapse of our marriage. I studied the subject above to some detail and used it to understand from this perspective to explore what faults occurred. From which I will explore why it happened and what I could have done to avoid it, and additionally, what I still can do to make sure history does not repeat itself. Some of us learn through experience, and some of us learn from mistakes created by us directly or indirectly. Nevertheless, after the collapse of something that was meant to last the full nine yards. I believe I needed to understand why and what went wrong, so I don't make the same mistake again.

So, here's what happened to me:

""What if this happens, if I do that.""

""what if that happens, if I do this.""

""This might happen if I do that. ""

""This might happen if I do this. ""

This is something taught at a young age at school for supposedly to maintain our wellbeing, but really it is the control some of us are handed to keep us guessing about our actions before some of us take action.

What I am talking about, you ask?

Well!!!

Worrying and how to root out the issues that bring this mindset to realization.

Something some of us have come to rely on, so some of us keep our mind occupied with unforeseen problems and circumstances which may never play out.

It is a tool that is passed from parent to child for generations.

There is, of course, good worrying and wrong worrying, which is fine within reason.

Still,

excessive worrying can bring other factors to light, such as high anxiety, high blood pressure, and stress, not mention health issues. Which can be life-threatening in some cases such as heart attacks.

My father is a constant worrier, and I have not only been trained on it but inherited this issue overly. It never used to bother me, but my partner pointed it out, and since then, it has become an ever-growing increasing concern.

She has never seen someone worry about so many little factors in life. I remember I use to say to my partner, ""you live in a merry little world, something out of a Dickens novel."

However, now I see, it wasn't that see worried less, it was me what worried excessively as I over thought about everything.

I would triple check things, and my partner would check once and be done with it.

I would be hysterical running around conducting security checks when we were going on vacation, and my partner would walk straight out of the door, seemingly with no care in the world. I would worry for the both of us, and in some ways, it made me feel whole because we were safe due to my insecurity issues.

"'the saying goes: the less I care, the happier I am.'"

Of course, because if some of us were careless, then some of us worry less, thus the happiness emerges through a calmer mind and not of a busier one.

<u>I remember a story about two monks who were walking towards a river, and they passed a woman who was struggling to get across the river with her shopping.</u>

The monks were forbidden to talk or touch women.

The older monk observed the situation and walked over to the woman and picked her up while handing the shopping bags to the younger monk.

As they crossed the river; the younger monk was worried that someone would see them; they would be punished.

Soon as they were on the other side, the older monk put the woman down and started walking, the younger monk gave the bags to the woman and started walking with his master.

After a while, the younger monk stopped and said to the older monk, ""what is going to happen to us, you broke the rules, and I cannot stop thinking about it, but you don't seem bothered""

The older monk, said, ""soon as some of us were on the other side of the river, I stopped worrying because I never broke the rules.

I didn't touch the woman, I picked her up as I would pick up a sack of potatoes, but you have been obsessing over this for almost the entire journey, some of us must learn to worry less and think more.

The moral of the story is that some of us think less and worry more, I find myself occasionally worrying about unforeseeable circumstances that may never come true.

Excessive worrying comes under a branch of OCD. It is where one's mind connects habitual thoughts to objects. Such security checks and turning off the light switches. The process typically needs to be repeated amount of times before the anxiety comes down. Sometimes excessive worrying can be misconstrued with security-conscious behaviour. If you are checking excessively meaning more than twice, then it may be the case that you are displaying outrageous worrying behaviour. Which can manifest into paranoia, which will evidently bring you to a halt? It will confuse your mind and trick you into submission anytime and anywhere you choose to do some sort of security checks.

For this type of issue, it may best to get some professional help. Because it is something that may manifest into depression as it is very closely linked to high anxiety issues.

Please check the indicators listed below:

The indicators

1. Excessive worrying and tension

2. Troubling thoughts

3. Excessive caring

4. An unrealistic view of problems

5. Feeling agitated

6. Restlessness

The solution

1. Stop late nights – late nights put unimaginable stress on the mind because nights are when the reason makes heads and tales of your issues in the day. So, sleep earlier and gain a better perspective in the morning.

2. Aromatherapy – The mind needs a relaxing time, a time where the reason can think about how to make your work more efficient. The

aroma has healing powers that interact with the mind. This is why aromatherapy is excellent to use, along with humidifiers, dehumidifiers, and oil defuses. The reason can have some 'me' time, and once it refreshes, you think better and make better decisions.

3. Yoga to ease tight pockets of muscles that have been gathering tension. Just like the mind needs time to recover, so does the body. The body has ways in which it needs to stretch out to work more efficiently. Yoga engages dormant muscles and gives rest to those overworked out muscles. While the tightness eases, you as a human start to feel a less stressful life. A life where you can do as you want without being restrained by the movement because you may have a seated job, and the body has become unresponsive to some areas while others' body parts are overtired.

5. Listen to forests, wale, and soothing sounds to ease the chatter of the mind. This helps bring the sense to attention; the mind needs time to process the daily downloaded information from what you observe and learn and what you stress about.

6. Write or compile your worries in words on paper, like I have done in some parts of this book. The words you write have power; think Shakespeare's words still have meaning in our lives. From which some of us adapt our lives each day, from which we can learn and become better.

Tips!!

1. Worrying less about those small cogs that some of us pay too much attention too. And end up in a stressful situation as a result. Think, the less you worry, the more you have a carefree life. Think,

can you control a situation? Why worry? Is the problem out of your control? Then why worry?

3. Careless - Step back and see, is your caring really needed at the advanced stage you are offering it?

4. Go on vacation – go somewhere you have never been once a year.

5. Overcome irritability – there comes the point in one's life when some of us must realize who has been there for us. Not the people who just say they care, but the people who actually have put themselves out for you. It is that time to close the doors on people who never mattered, who, more importantly, bring out your irritable side. It is time to only have people in your life that only risk it all for you. Keep

your circle small with positive, optimistic people who bring out the good in you.

6. Stop worrying about other people's issues – stop being contrived with other people's problems over your own. Because there comes the point where you may cross the line of caring for someone and start to fix their problems, which indirectly their issues have just become yours. Stop, listen to people, stop think; gather your thoughts on the matter and think about what you have to gain by worrying for someone else. That's not helping, that's doing their job for them. How will they ever learn to be reliant on you? Unburden yourself and detach from other people's problems. Helping and caring are noble, but sometimes some people end up becoming a part of the problem and trying to remedy something they don't need to. Don't adopt other people's problems.

My prayer

Bless me, my Gods, & Goddesses, please grant me a partner to share the road ahead and children to brighten up our journey with laughter and memories, which I pray for each day, in my heart of hearts.

Chapter 13 – compulsion, & abandonment

Based on my past conversations, I believe I have ascertained unique perspectives surrounding the above issue. I Believe I have understood my situation a little better since the worst happened by analysing my last marriage. I did this by exploring critical conversations between my partner and me by examining the necessary details that lead up to the collapse of our marriage. I studied the subject above to some detail and used it to understand from this perspective to explore what faults occurred. From which I will explore why it happened and what I could have done to avoid it, and additionally, what I still can do to make sure history does not repeat itself. Some of us learn through experience, and some of us learn from mistakes created by us directly or indirectly. Nevertheless, after the collapse of something that was meant to last the full nine yards. I believe I needed to understand why and what went wrong, so I don't make the same mistake again.

So, here's what happened to me:

Chapter 9 – Compulsion

Based on my past conversations, I believe I have ascertained unique perspectives surrounding the above issue. I Believe I have understood my situation a little better since the worst happened by analysing my last marriage. I did this by exploring critical conversations between my partner and me by examining the necessary details that lead up to the collapse of our marriage. I studied the subject above to some detail and used it to understand from this perspective to explore what faults occurred. From which I will explore why it happened and what I could have done to avoid it, and additionally, what I still can do to make sure history does not repeat itself. Some of us learn through experience, and some of us learn from mistakes created by us directly or indirectly.

Nevertheless, after the collapse of something that was meant to last the full nine yards. I believe I needed to understand why and what went wrong, so I don't make the same mistake again.

So, here's what happened to me:

I saw the Vampire Diaries (2010) and realized that compulsion is a real thing, although the episodes are fiction, with vampires trying to control people through compelling them to do their bidding.

I have a side-splitting feeling that I had this condition because I had trouble saying 'NO' to some people. It is like a feeling in my gut that is wrenching me to do something I don't want to. No matter how much I resist, I end up doing it anyway, it's like I am compelled to assist another. Sometimes even if the other person hasn't even asked for my help, I do it always.

This is, so, difficult for me; no matter how hard I try, I give in; it's like something or someone has a hold on me, and somehow, they can override my decisions. For example, when my partner would ask me to do something, and I 'declined,' my partner would send me on a guilt trip.

However, there were other scenarios whereby I might have misconstrued compulsion for a favour, I dunno!

Any who,

Scenario one

I used to pride myself on having the ability to do things outside the boundaries of societal understanding. It was like I would remember to do more things for the person that I'm helping than they initially asked. I've put this down to what I call 'investment favours.'

Bear with me for a moment,

'Investment favours' are something that I would do for somebody expecting somebody to do for me as I have for them, with the interest of course.

As I'm doing the favour, should something else arise, perhaps an extra job I haven't been asked to do? I would go ahead and complete the favour and everything else that came along with it, thus turning a single favour into a multitude of endorsements. In my mind, I have done the above and beyond for the person. So, I expect a return on my favours bigger than what I gave. Because I had to make adjustments to the favour that was asked of me, so, in essence, each time I have to make an adjustment that becomes another favour which I am doing for the person.

Let me humour you for a second because this part is tricky to follow.

I would expect a significant return on my; investment favours, but the other person would only see one favour. So, when it comes to returning the favour. To me, it would be like the stock market just collapsed because the colossal favour the time was expecting was not acknowledged by the other side because I never told them exactly what I did for them.

For some odd reason, I assume that they are aware of the lengths that I went to in completing the favour that they asked of me. Without having an agreement in place of what the person owes me. I assume they would concede, or perhaps someone in their association educated them in terms of what I did for them, I dunno!

So, investment favours piled up, and when it came time to cash them in. Some people have forgotten, while others don't even remember agreeing to return the favours because, in their eyes, it was something very trivial. From that point on, I start to resent the situation. And being that there was a multitude of problems. I have managed to emotionally prison myself within my mind because I can't understand why some people don't know that it is a give-and-take situation. Not a one-way street.

Any who,

Scenario two

Sometimes I find myself lost in translation because I have difficulty trying to talk to two-faced people. Because I never know which face, I'm talking to, haha.

Since two-faced people tend to become your best friend and then all of a sudden, they're not. Because I am a sincere and honest person, I take people at face value, so if somebody tells me this is how it is, I have no reason to doubt them.

As far back as I can remember, it has always been the same. In terms of people would use me to do a job, and then if something goes wrong, they turn around and tell people that they didn't even ask me to do it.

For example, we went to this wedding, and I was told to inform the person in charge that they were running out of liquor.

When I approach the person in charge, they said to me, "what are you talking about" I reiterated what I was told even louder than needed and not to mention in front of the guests.

So, when the person asked me "who told you this," I pointed out the person who told me, of course, the person denied it, they simply pointed out that perhaps I had too much to drink.

The other person merely wanted to embarrass me and look grandiose over me. I suppose!

However, my anxiety would go up, and I would act erratically and cause a scene, perhaps even a dispute which ends up in some antisocial behaviour. Because I would just feed into whatever they were dishing out. Never realizing why!

Any who,

Scenario three

When are used to take on tasks, are used to do everything myself, and for some odd reason, I would never get applause, not even a tap on the back for doing a top job? However, soon as there was a problem, all of a sudden, some people were happy to give me the blame.

There comes the point in one's life when we must simply state "<u>enough is enough</u>"

So, I stopped going to family functions and anywhere else because I feared some people setting me up for a fall.

I thought people respected me, but really, they just laughed at me; I became the jester at the parties often.